MADE
TO MARKET

Marketing in a World
Focused on Sales

SARAH STAHL

Published in the United States by Ingram Spark

First Print Edition, 2021

Edited by Julie Sykora

Cover design and typesetting by Jennifer Blair

Author Photograph by Life's Mirror Images

ISBN 978-0-578-95801-9

To,
My Husband Daniel,
Our children Abigail, John & Hannah—
along with everyone who believed
in me along the way!

Thank you, Xoxo Sarah

FORWARD

I had a passion for designing stationery and a desire to start my own business. I knew my target customers, but had no clue how to actually reach them. One day after answering an unknown phone call, who could have ever imagined that my life would completely change. On the other end of that phone call was the one and only… Sarah Stahl. That call was the first step in making my entrepreneurial dreams become a profitable reality.

Sarah and I had similar entrepreneurial passions and skills that afforded us the ability to collaborate and grow our businesses in ways we could have ever imagined. What made Sarah's approach to business unique, was her ability to constantly evolve and understand the methodology of the customer.

Marketing is the backbone of Sarah Stahl's DNA. As a business partner and friend of Sarah for over 10 years, I have watched Sarah transform businesses through her logical and common sense approach to marketing. She has always been a leader in the field even when she didn't realize her phenomenal impact on the industry. She has led successful marketing campaigns in numerous industry sectors such as commercial real estate, tourism, non-profit, and ecommerce just to name a few. Her marketing strategies are built on solid business principles that she lives by and can be applied across the board.

Sarah is witty and smart and everything she touches comes to life. As a loving wife, mother, and thought-leader she embodies the experience and knowledge to guide you on this marketing journey. So sit back and enjoy the ride as this book navigates you through the wild world of MARKETING.

Temisha Mitchell Young
Managing Partner, Avant Creative
Temisha@avant-creative.com

CONTENTS

REFERENCES

Agorapulse

American Marketing Association

Alex Cattoni

Andrew Davis

Business 2 Business

Brandon Cox

Chelsea Peitz

Cliff Ravenscraft

Convince & Convert

Canva

Chris Mercer

Chris Erthel

Crystal Vilkaitis

Danielle Wiley

Etsy

Emeric Ernoult

Faulkner University

Frank Cespedes

Gary Vaynerchuk

Helen Blunden

HubSpot

Incare Technology

Kimba Cooper

Landra Lynn Jacobs

LEGO

Marie Forleo

Merrilee Hale

Mitzi Eaker

Mark Schaefer

Marketing Charts

Marketing Land

Mark McCrindle

Neil Patel

Poo-Pourri

Rand Fishkin

Social Media Examiner

Sandy Carter

The Social Dilemma

The Age of Surveillance Capitalism

The University of Florida

Ready to get started?
Let's jump into what it takes to get you
or your organization "made to market" ready.

INTRODUCTION

I don't know anyone who grew up saying, "I'm going to be a marketer one day!"

When I was growing up, I couldn't even utter an articulate answer to the question, "Who do you want to be when you grow up?" I was born in Nashua, New Hampshire but grew up in a Florida household that fostered zero forethought into what adulthood might bring. I had no clue what I wanted to do when I left home. In fact, most of my childhood memories are spotty, and that's probably for the best.

What do I remember? Raking!

As a pre-teen with four siblings who shared a three-bedroom, one-and-a-half bath rental with our parents, I spent my summers raking. You may not believe that a Florida yard had enough to keep me busy all summer, but then you've never had pine trees! A family of seven living on the poverty line didn't offer many options for extracurricular activities when school was out.

No school meant you could find me in the yard under the hot Florida sun. Often, I dared to imagine someone actually acknowledging the work I'd put into the half-acre lot where our woodsy neighborhood ended. But no such reality ever unfolded. Still, I believed in my mantra with all my heart: "The better job I do, the better the reward I'll get!"

So, I worked harder, raked longer, and even tried to find free ways to make the yard — sparkle.

Nobody ever stopped by to recognize the "world's best yard," but for some reason, I never stopped believing that it would happen — someday. And so, my relentless passion and reckless abandon over what I thought possible was born!

As I grew older, my relentless passion shifted from yard manicuring to business, something else I knew absolutely nothing about. I was not the girl playing with dolls and dreaming of my wedding day. When I wasn't raking, I was the girl building forts and dreaming of owning a bed and breakfast. As it turned out, a natural inclination for business is the perfect accompaniment for the marketing profession.

But that didn't come to light until the eve of my 30th birthday. Yup, I'm one of those peculiar (old) millennials who didn't find my place or purpose in the world until stumbling my way through life for the better part of two decades. Literally,

I stumbled hard into one of the most creatively rewarding professional roles on the planet: marketer. Or, as Sandy Carter, VP of Amazon Web Services, calls us — marketeers!

Why is it we ask young kids to tell us what they want to be when they're older? They don't know! Still, we see more stereotypical professions like doctor, lawyer, vet, or sports star depicted in childhood play. Yet, in 2019, the U.S. saw 314,900 available marketing jobs with a projected expansion of 7% more marketing jobs before 2029. In contrast, 2019 offered 112,000 vet positions, 813,000 law positions, and 738,000 medical-related positions. And while roughly 480,000 athletes compete in the NCAA, just a select few within each sport moved on to compete at the professional or even Olympic level.

According to the Bureau of Labor Statistics, 25 occupational groups make up over 250 career choices, and one of the fastest-growing is marketing management. Considering this demand for marketing professionals forecasted smack-dab in the middle of the three professions most commonly depicted during childhood play, why is the marketing industry still so elusive? Is it because marketing is so often confused with sales or advertising? Although participation numbers may suggest marketing is as well understood as any other profession, that's not how job descriptions, career expectations, or professional stepping stones have played out in a profession solely responsible for business growth in every major industry within the past hundred years.

Often made up of some of the most technically-trained professionals, marketers can make over six digits a year but are frequently among the first positions cut during an economic downturn.

So is the profession important or not?

It's valued enough to pay well but not enough to keep around in a tight spot. Yet, the reality for the marketing industry is that it's the only profession that has a hand in elevating the success of every business on planet earth! No other profession can boast holistic business healing capabilities, regardless of business sector.

Next time you run across someone not in the marketing space, ask them —

"Can you tell me what a marketer does in 10 words or less?"

Heck, you may even be a marketer and struggle with this one. Now, ask a follow-up question to see how easily they can articulate the roles of lawyers, doctors, or vets using the same amount of words.

Try it, and you'll see my point!

Business leaders understand that marketing is important but have trouble articulating any true value proposition. They assume it's the fans they earn from a new social media presence, or ad views after a successful negotiation, the new content on their updated website, or the networking that happened at the last Chamber of Commerce function. Although those all have their place in marketing, I often see organizations focusing on incoherent activities in their marketing execution with no fundamental understanding of its role in the long-term business growth and development process.

I know, frustrating, right? I agree, and it's among the core reasons that compelled me to write this book. Before it's all said and done, I will lay a path forward during a time when marketing is in the midst of a technology-driven evolution. Yes, an evolution because the future of marketing is not in quick hacks; it's in mastering the tasks that made the industry a foundational necessity in the first place.

> ## "Marketing is the management of profitable relationships."

My marketing journey has inspired every human emotion in me—from perplexing disappointment to surprising success—a journey you'll relate to and hopefully be encouraged by.

During my decade-long stumble into a Director of Marketing position, the marketing industry was never really on my radar. An entrepreneur to my core (although I consider myself a failed entrepreneur, but we'll get to that later), it was a deep interest in business development paired with a love for outdoor adventure that slowly tangled its way through my life, culminating into my most recent position as the Director of Marketing & Tourism in the Mountain Lake Region of Northeast Alabama. Here, everything finally came together for me, and I want to tell you how and why.

My journey reveals what goes on behind the scenes to revolutionize marketing in the digital age. I'll also share my story of the heartache, disappointments, failures, and plain-old shenanigans—the price I paid to arrive at this point in my life — to set you on a smoother, straightforward path on your journey to becoming a respected marketing professional.

As of this writing in 2021, I've been in the marketing space for nearly a decade. As my expertise deepens, so does my frustration over two glaring facts plaguing the industry. So, let's start there!

1. The Sales vs. Marketing Debacle

Colleagues may think I'm crazy to even address this age-old debate. But, the misinformation plaguing the marketing space that prevents businesses from reaching their true potential keeps me up at night! For that reason alone, I must be quiet no longer. To keep it short and sweet—it's a hot mess! Have you ever applied for a job described as a "marketing opportunity," only to discover it was really a sales position? If that's the case, then you've personally experienced this major flaw, perhaps without even realizing it. It's debilitating to marketing careers—diluting the power of marketing—during the most pivotal time in the history of business longevity.

Consider this for a moment. As a culture, consumers don't want to be sold to, right? Then why do companies think hiring more sales positions will improve declining business performance? It's madness! If people don't want to be sold to—statistics point to this daily—then why do we continue to see increases in sales staff and a decrease in marketing staff?

The fact is, the lines between sales and marketing are severely blurred, but I'll draw clear and concise lines between the two, at long last.

Pro tip to employers: It's actually insulting to take a well-rounded marketing resume and try to stuff it into a square sales position. We'll get into the mind, mission, and training behind marketing later, but let's cut to the chase—marketers are not built for sales. They are built to manage and develop forward-thinking, competitive message positioning to solidify and execute a brand's corporate identity. In fact, the magic of marketing is its ability to execute savvy storytelling and digital communications that result in increased leads for your sales team.

If you're finding that hard to believe, I encourage you to read on before making a final judgment.

2. The Knowledge Gap Dilemma

Why are marketers so focused on social media alone? Why are they obsessed with beating the algorithms and growth hacking their way into vanity metrics like increased follower count? Marketers have fallen victim to shiny new tools that fall short in connecting customers with the valuable solutions they seek. The knowledge gap between understanding a well-rounded marketing mix and social-only solutions is just as crippling as the blurred lines of sales and marketing.

But who's even talking about it?

Yeah, social media is hands-down the best tool marketers have ever had to communicate a strong brand message and interact directly with customers. But social media is just a stop on the customer journey. The way I see it, it's like inviting a new friend to your home but never inviting them to step in off the porch. The porch is an excellent place for short and sweet chats, but friendships are made in the den over a glass of wine and deep conversations.

Today, we depend on social media "porch chats" to win customers without taking the time and effort to have those "deep den conversations." That's where we are today, but how did we get here? We can't know where we've strayed unless we know where we've been, so let's take a look at how marketing evolved over the years.

Marketing's humble beginnings were simply about how to better present goods for competition purposes. The early twentieth century to the late 1940s brought increased competition to the business world. Increasing sales through marketing techniques became an essential part of the competitive landscape. As a result, brand development and monitoring of market value became a standard business practice.

That's when the business world was first introduced to the creative depth of marketing. Savvy messages emerged, negotiation for ad spaces began, and the design and delivery process became paramount. Once a project was complete, marketers merely moved on to the next project as calls poured into the sales team.

Not to downplay the marketing challenges back in the day, but considering what marketers have to know and execute today, that short-list sounds like a dream come true! Seriously, if you haven't seen a job description for a marketing manager or related position, it'll make your head spin.

Take a look!

- Bachelor's Degree, Master's preferred

- 10 years of marketing experience, preferably within an agency

- Strong written and spoken communication skills

- Analytical skills a must!

Okay, not too bad a start, but we are far from done!

- Guide company staff to integrate marketing strategies across multiple social platforms, creating a balanced marketing mix

- Leverage real-time analytics to fine-tune marketing content across multiple consumer touchpoints, both on and offline

- Develop forward-thinking market and competitive positioning to solidify & execute the brand's corporate identity

- Author web-optimized press releases, resulting in media run stories

- Conduct competitor analysis to increase marketplace positioning

- Set up & manage targeted advertising both online and off

- Superior speaking, content writing, relationship-building, networking, and customer service skills

- Serve as a spokesperson and lead point on media interactions that help promote and impact organizational growth

- Experience with team-based product development that resulted in increased sales performance

- Optimize analytic capabilities to track visitor web behavior

- Analyze web metrics such as time on site, page views per visit, transaction volume and revenue, click-through rates, CPA+PPC, and other analytic functions to determine ROI

- Develop and implement integrated strategic marketing and communications plan

- Run highly targeted social media ads that lead users through a digital sales funnel

- Create PR agency-level graphic designs using industry-standard software

- Manage web, multimedia, and art design staff to create websites and other digital content related to visual branding

We're still far from done, but you get the point. That list wraps up over ten years of software, web development, customer service, public relations, analytical, social media, graphic design, and team management experience.

From an employer's perspective, and rightfully so, a marketer's skills span way beyond social media.

But are marketers learning all of this? Are they being exposed to it? And if so, is the professional development process teaching marketers how to connect all the dots in the overall brand development process? Not only must marketers know and understand the above list, but we must also have the expertise to differentiate between how these skills are used to market and how they're used during a story-based promotion process that works in tandem with the sales staff.

With a bachelor's degree, students learn two years of their craft but need 5-10 years of experience to land a legit position. With a master's, it's up to four years of study, but still not quite meeting the experience threshold employers expect.

I went to college at 30 and earned a Bachelor of Business Administration from Faulkner University. I went on to get a Master of Science Marketing from Southern New Hampshire University to fill in gaps during my real-world training years. I am a Certified Social Media Marketing Professional through the University of Florida and hold Google Analytics and HubSpot Inbound Marketing Certifications. I'm just creeping up on my ten-year mark in the industry, yet I've been told only once that I qualify for a full-time position in the marketing field!

I don't know Photoshop, I'm not an Excel whiz, I cannot code, I don't have a strong sales background, and I've only used a handful of the hundreds of customer relationship management (CRM) tools that many companies use. But, as a master communicator, savvy storyteller, and relentless analytics observer, somehow, I've managed to accomplish everything in this book as a business owner, freelance marketer and now, director of marketing over the course of ten years.

That's all to say that according to employers' expectations, I barely qualify for a marketing position. Yet, here I am ten years into a thriving career that brings me as much joy as my children do.

I'm going to tell you how you can experience that same level of fulfillment in marketing. Not only how but why you should pursue your career in marketing.

As a marketer, you'll not only learn the steps and acquire the technical skills and insight, but you'll also be equipped to combat the naysayers that may be holding you back.

For employers, you'll better understand how marketers operate, what they are trained to accomplish and how to staff these vital roles within your organization.

The main point of this book is all about reframing foundational marketing principles by understanding:

- Who's filling the knowledge gap to ensure the marketing craft is effectively developed in organizations?

- Who's guiding organizational leaders, managers, and executives from resorting to doubling down on sales efforts as a panic move because their marketing isn't working?

- Who's ensuring the next generation of marketers is better than us?

- Who's encouraging our kids to be more than just the fab four they seem all too aware of?

The truth is, we live in a world where kids do pretend to be marketers—they just don't know it! They're playing the role of creative storytellers, visual design artists, YouTubers, coders, data scientists, and Instagram divas while unknowingly practicing for a successful career in marketing. Whether for a company or themselves.

It's time we encourage generations of marketers to embrace the power of the only profession responsible for elevating the success of every business on the planet! In this book, you'll not only find that answer, but you'll also find the tools, technical know-how, and path forward to develop yourself and your organization to practice better marketing habits in an ever-changing consumer-driven landscape.

Ready to get started?

Let's jump into what it takes to get you or your organization "Made to Market" ready.

Chapter 1

WHAT IS MARKETING, ANYWAY?

Think about how multi-faceted we are as humans. We've got these quirks and preferences that shape who we are and define our place in the world. Consider a marketer's traits. If you have a boundless curiosity around business, are fascinated by the nuances of human psychology, have a culturally active and accepting brain, an often-smiling face accompanied by exceptional communication and analytical skills, you may be destined for marketing. If I just described you, and you're not sure what you want to be when you grow up, let me assure you, you'll make a great marketer!

We know we're not supposed to judge people based on first impressions. But we all do it! And when we do, we get it wrong most of the time because we lack insight into all of that person's dimensions, the parts that make them whole. But as we develop a relationship with them and peel back the layers, we begin to realize what's beneath the surface. We have a better sense of why they're indispensably valued in the world and deserve to be treated as such. You know how when you fall in love with somebody, and you think they're the best thing since sliced bread and you can't fathom why the rest of the world doesn't see what you see?

That's how marketers look at people.

It's not a matter of "They aren't like me; I'm out of here!" It's, "If I could understand them better, my life and the life of those around me could improve." Marketers typically have a heart and soul to serve others and care deeply for their co-workers, customers, and communities. So, time and effort are often spent on knowing people better with an open mind to improve humanity in some way.

These empathetic souls dedicate themselves to organizations for one reason: to bridge the human-to-business connectivity gap. Without them, business will always suffer. Why? Because business is about people, and marketers are trained to skillfully communicate while explicitly influencing their fellow humans.

What is Marketing?

Literally, take a moment to write some of your ideas on what marketing is to you in the notes section of this chapter.

If you had a hard time pinning down a definition, welcome to the crowd! It's no surprise that the concept of marketing is elusive. Its lack of structural standards is a cause for confusion in its own space. For this reason, we need to retrain ourselves to approach marketing from the foundational construct that originally built the industry to function in valuable ways we've now strayed from. That's what this book is all about!

Understanding why we market first requires us to understand what marketing is. I like to work on solid ground to build strong foundations, so let's first point out what it's not—to rule out those pesky perceptions that cloud "real" marketing.

Marketing is NOT:

Sales
Hard
Customer Service
Graphic Arts
Crisis Management
Senior Management's personal publicity machine
Human Resources
A quick fix for failing products
Sales! Yes, it's important enough to mention twice on the same list.

Let's face it, to the average businessperson, marketing equals promotional advertisement and anything that resembles it. But, to better understand the original philosophies behind marketing, think about the movie *Around the World in 80 Days*. The 1956 story is about a Victorian Englishman who bets that he can circumnavigate the globe using new steamships and railways in just 80 days. Neat, right? That's marketing. It used an influencer-based public relations stunt that sold cutting-edge travel options to the tech-leery consumer.

Think *Harvard Business Review* for more marketing foundations. A branded product solely owned and operated by Harvard University began in 1922 as an elite microeconomics journal for students and business professionals. Today, it's one of the most widely known and well-respected business periodicals in the world. Responsible not just for an additional revenue stream but also for leveraging the school as one of the most elite business colleges known to man.

Both resulted in a sales increase that altered the construct of the world's economy in life-changing ways. However, the act of selling did not make those stunts marketing; it was the long-term, consistent, consumer touchpoints that developed reliability- resulting in magnificent outcomes.

> "When you take the burden to sell
> out of the equation, marketing thrives,
> and business multiplies."

Sales is NOT Marketing

Sales is typically defined as the exchange of a commodity for money. It's the closing of a deal, resulting in a financial interchange. Sales is the more intimate interaction responsible for brokering relationships with potential clients with the goal of providing a solution that will eventually lead to a sale — the customer's personal "handler," if you will.

Marketing is NOT Sales

Marketing involves calculated storytelling to create communication outlets that connect customers, clients, partners and influence societal mindsets. Marketing-focused communications influence consumer spending, and enhance a company's reputation through target audience identification. Communication with a defined audience is then consistent, professional, and ongoing. In short, it's the process of getting people interested in the goods and services that may be sold to them at another point in time.

I lead the horse to water. – Marketing

I cause the horse to drink it. – Sales

It's marketing *and* sales, not marketing *or* sales, or even marketing as sales. I certainly don't want to widen the professional divide, as both departments need each other fiercely! But somewhere, the marketing industry lost clarity. How? Well, if I had to choose a single reason why marketing has lost its effectiveness, clout, and respectability over the years, it's because marketing has been grossly confused with sales, and we're not really doing a whole lot about it.

Now that we know what marketing isn't, let's talk about what it is.

A clear and well-communicated benefit.
Advocating for a well-defined three-dimensional customer.
The helpful tasks your organization engages in to provide value to your community and your customers.
Respect and relationships built with customers.
The systematically thought out and calculated steps that lead customers through an on-boarding process.
The story told about your brand's identity and how it relates to your customer's pain points.
Distinct and defined business processes that lead to growth and credibility over a long period of time.
Making sense of data that leads to clarified business decisions and long-term growth.
Visual creativity applied consistently across all brand pieces.
The ongoing message about a customer's journey.
The ongoing management of profitable relationships.
Instant brand recognition.

Here's what the tangibles look like:

A brand kit,
A website,

A corporate magazine,

Newsletters,

Brochures,

Direct mailers,

Posters,

Business cards,

Signage,

Social media content,

Inbound marketing communications,

A podcast,

A YouTube channel,

Digital banners

Even a book.

That's right; I'm marketing to you right now! Not to be confused with selling, I'm not trying to get you to buy anything; you've already done that. I am, however, building trust, earning your respect and a place in your mind where you may consider me a knowledgeable voice in this space. Maybe, one day you'll reach out to ask a question or offer me consulting work or even a job. Maybe I'll just become a trusted marketing resource you tap into from time to time during your own career.

That's fine. That's marketing! Marketing is what you say and how you say it, when and where you explain what you provide, and why people should take notice. Okay, not a succinct definition but clear at least. That may not be the only reason you've committed to a few hours of interim education and honest storytelling, but I can promise you that all the frustration you feel over marketing is why I decided to tackle this topic. I share those frustrations with you, and I want to do something about it!

Talk About Changes!

The business world has changed! Covid-19 exposed the cracks and sped up the need to innovate, and it's way past time for marketing to play catch-up! It's time to realize and leverage the full potential of marketing's hibernating talent, foundational structure, and power to transform businesses across the globe.

You've already seen it in action. Think about brands like Coke, Amazon, Geico, Starbucks, or Apple. How did you feel when you read those names? If you can articulate a feeling, you are a recipient of the power of brand marketing. Unfortunately, the number-one holdup in creating an equally powerful brand presence for most business owners today is a total misdirection of long-term marketing focus.

The transformation process starts with taking marketing seriously in your own organization. Have you tried to lose weight recently? If you have, how committed were you to the long-term consistency needed to see noticeable results? Or did you try some new wonder program that you quit a month later due to lack of results? Marketing is not a quick fix to an intermittent sales dip. And wonder marketing will not provide the fix you're seeking. It's the long-term management of profitable relationships that engages the brand to elicit the buying feelings that Coke, Amazon, Geico, Starbucks, or Apple can conjure.

We all know a thing or two about the complexity of what it takes to see lasting and authentic weight-loss results. The same thinking applies to marketing. So, if you haven't already started your organization's marketing transformation process, you're already way behind the curve. The good news is you can still catch up! In this book, we'll cut through the confusion and chaos preventing you from fostering continuous organizational growth.

Readers and Principles

I had two types of readers in mind when I wrote this book:

Marketers: New and seasoned marketers who want technical, strategic answers that lead to becoming a talented and respected career professional who can account for tangible growth in your organization. In this book, I discuss what you didn't learn in school and answer the questions to fill the gaps that may be preventing you from moving forward.

I address the changing industry and how to better understand its roots, including how to stay ahead of the evolution process. I address ethics, analytics, the skills gap, and strategic errors that dilute the industry's ability to accomplish true marketing potential. Then, I lay out essential basic skills all marketers should possess now—most of which revolve around an interconnected and measurable storytelling and content stacking process.

Employers: To employers in any industry who either feel lost on who to hire or want to create a more consistent hiring process to maximize your marketing department's performance. Here you will learn to better understand roles and the part they play in your growth process to ensure effective decision-making when hiring full-time or contract employees for a marketing-related position. Every year, it's more evident that choosing the right hire in this field is critical to organizational success. Your days of choosing blindly are over! I reveal technical skills that good marketers should possess to help you better understand how marketers should be functioning and their relational ties to your sales team. You've got a taste of that already, but if you're looking to organize your current marketing staff better and hire true marketers, read on. When you're finished, your approach to hiring a marketer will be totally different.

Marketers, in both instances, this content will cut through the confusing industry related clutter —making your career path much easier!

Additionally, I'd like you to know upfront the two hot topics I won't even touch.

1. This book is NOT for growth hackers

I have no plans to address or discuss shortcuts or cheat codes on how to circumvent your way to becoming a better marketer. Marketing is a learned skill with many moving parts, not a quick way to make a buck. This, in my opinion, is another reason the industry suffers, and I will not contribute to the madness.

2. This book will NOT teach manipulation

Marketing skirts this line too often all by itself due to the nature of the work and its relationship to the human psyche. I have no plans to discuss how to unethically manipulate or influence consumers into achieving your desired outcome. Ethics will be discussed, but it will be left to the reader to decide where they fall on the scale and how to make improved ethical decisions moving forward.

Truth be Told

As a human known for dropping "truth bombs—I have a reputation for keeping it real. Some like it, some don't. Nevertheless, the truth will be told.

The very first truth that comes to mind—and one we can all agree on—is that this life goes quickly! Now on the eve of my 40s, I'm called a "baby" quite a bit. Living in the South, they say it's somehow a compliment. But my Northern brain has to convince me of that… often. I mean, my babies are getting ready to graduate, so I can hardly claim the title.

What I can claim is a deep-rooted sense of perspective because I've been warned that "life goes quick, enjoy it" consistently since I was 19. Thankfully, I had the foresight to actually listen. I listened because I trusted others who had lived some life. So early on, I understood my kids would leave the house, and I would be dead before I knew it.

How's that for a truth bomb?

Let's Take a Moment to Talk About... Death

I think about death quite a bit. In the hopes of not totally bumming you out before you even make it past Chapter 1, it's essential to gain perspective on where you are and where you're heading on your own path.

I'm curious, do you ever think about death?

Not the fear of it or obsessing over how it will happen, but the reality of "I may not be here tomorrow, and if I get the chance to live a full life, will anyone remember the contributions I made to the world?"

Considering the sheer volume of people who've passed on since earth's creation compared to how many you recall, never-mind impacted you, the odds of being remembered aren't in our favor. I know that's a sober and profound start, but I'm a firm believer that we can't move forward until we understand where we are now. I want to help you advance in your career, and the reality is work and life are highly interconnected.

That's all to say, I urge you to fully understand where you are now to gain perspective on the "how and why" fueling your next best steps. To feel confident about your way forward, I'd like to share part of my life's recipe: a healthy dose of perspective.

You are so much more than just a marketer, and your career affects more than just your professional life. Considering the swiftness of life allows me to be more content with where I am today. Trust me, I have in no way perfected that statement, but I work on it daily. Whether in the midst of family chaos or working out a year-long marketing strategy, the impermanence of life gives me confidence in who I am today. It also enables me to carefully consider where I am in every moment of every day, including that last interchange with an annoying co-worker.

I could offer up a myriad of examples of the granular contributors this mindset has on my daily choices, but the point is, I strive to seize every daily opportunity with the hopes of living a life that glorifies God and impacts others now! This philosophy provides a fearlessness and the ability to seize opportunities that I may not have otherwise taken. It's what gave me hope while raking all summer long, and it's why I have the guts to write a book on a topic that thousands of other people are also experts in. It allows me to make things right between those I have offended and take career risks that could make or break me. In my mind, I have nothing to lose, and when your heart and intentions are pure, neither do you.

I get it; it's weird to talk about death in the first chapter of a marketing book, but here I am, seizing an opportunity to encourage you to look at your career relative to your life and what you hope to accomplish with both.

Why?

Because the path you take in life is important to me. If we looked at life as a roadmap, it would seem hectic—a hot mess of clumpy pavement laid down way too quick, not reaching any real destination. If we looked at life compared to someone else, we'd give up all hope of accomplishment because trust me, there's always someone better!

Made to Market

When we look to our life to validate who we are as humans, we'll always be left disappointed and wanting more. So, let's not look at life that way anymore! Instead, what if we looked at our life's path with a unique purpose? That your life is a combination of events that present opportunities to positively affect the lives of others.

What if our career isn't only about the work but also about the impact we're meant to leave on the world while leveraging the passions we've had since childhood? What if we were fully content with being as good as we are today, knowing we will learn, gain wisdom, and improve as we plod along?

If you are here to learn more about marketing, the next thought may be, "How can marketing have a lasting impact on my life? On any life?" Trust me, if that's what your calling is—you WILL make a lasting impact on many lives! The world tells us that the only way to make an impact is to engage in sweeping, heroic sacrifices that end in practical knighthood. But what if each of our lives is precisely that? Sacrificial. Without all the pomp and circumstance, of course.

I mean, I'd prefer NOT to be knighted, or whatever the female version is. That kind of attention just makes me feel very uncomfortable, anyway! But what if our impact is in the generational stories passed down among the progeny of those we've impressed ourselves upon? I'd much rather focus on that because who knows how the world will spin it. At least in the latter scenario, it's a genuine response to the real impact of walking a mile with another human. Severely lacking in our present world, a service-based life is way more rewarding than knighthood and at the core of a true marketer.

I believe each life is special, has a purpose, and is meant to be used to glorify God. Even if you are a marketer. When we glorify God, we aren't the ones taking credit, but our lives are a reflection of His work in us. My husband puts it much better, mostly because, as a screenwriter, he's much better at storytelling than I am. When I'm highly discouraged, have no clue why I'm drawn to marketing and can't fathom why I'm so passionate about it—losing sleep over solutions to problems I dream about solving—Dan says, "If you are a street sweeper, sweep streets to the glory of God." Then he'll go on to say, "If you are a marketer, market to the glory of God."

So, I wake up today the same way I wake up every day—Made to Market for the glory of God.

NOTES

Chapter 2

EVERYONE'S A MARKETER

Lots of "Marketers," Little Performance

You may have noticed the marketing industry is heavily saturated yet under-performing. In short, this means there are way too many people claiming to be marketing experts in marketing roles and performing marketing tasks without producing real results indicative of successful marketing performance.

True marketing is a function of roughly ten role sectors, with a combination of varying skills — to get the work done. Marketing is a collaborative discipline by nature, so there will always be some overlap between roles. Perhaps that's why different organizations use a plethora of assorted job titles for marketing roles, so we'll keep it on the simple side.

In the annual marketing report conducted by Social Media Examiner — 2020 results revealed that out of 5,243 marketing professionals who participated in their survey, 65% indicated having 3 years or less of experience in the career field and holding titles like:

- Social Media Marketing Manager

- Marketing Consultant

- Marketing Manager

- Marketing Director

- Marketing Analyst

- Marketing Coordinator

- Marketing Specialist

- Communications Director

- Promotions Manager

- Ads Manager

The list goes on, but from an uninformed organizational leadership perspective, do you know the difference in marketing functions between these titles? For someone not in the industry, each title has no differentiation, no true distinction, and is considered interchangeable by many organizational leaders. Yet somehow, these roles are thought to behold the "next best" business solution with little idea as to how.

So, how will leaders recognize the difference between these roles and their effect on the organization? As professional marketers, that education is now our responsibility because organizational growth depends on it.

A Marketer's Duty

If you hold one of these roles, you carry the burden of guiding leadership in the right direction — from the hiring process and beyond. This duty as a marketer is clearly defined among marketing pledges associated with organizational excellence through codes of conduct similar to The American Marketing Association's initiating pledge:

> "*As Marketers, we must: Do no harm. This means consciously avoiding harmful actions or omissions by embodying high ethical standards and adhering to all applicable laws and regulations in the choices we make by fostering trust in the marketing system. This means striving for good faith and fair dealing so as to contribute toward the efficacy of the exchange process as well as avoiding deception in product design, pricing, communication, and delivery of distribution. Embrace ethical values.*"

But as marketers, we haven't even figured out that it's against Facebook Community Guidelines to host a giveaway on a newsfeed. Never mind how we should handle an ethical situation like Volkswagen faced in 2015. In a scandal dubbed "Diesel Dupe," the automobile giant marketed eco-friendly vehicles that emitted nitrogen oxide pollutants up to 40 times above what's allowed in the U.S. This wreaked havoc across the company, crippling their brand image and marketing messaging in ways from which the organization is still working to recover. Unfortunately, today's marketers don't seem prepared for either of these two very real scenarios.

So, what do the accomplishments of a proficient marketer look like?

- Clearly articulated target audience profiles

- Increased brand exposure

- Increase web traffic

- Generated leads

- Developed and grew a loyal fan base

- Improved sales pipeline

- Grew business partnerships

- Provided marketplace insight

- Increased thought leadership

- Communicated effectively with the media

- Articulated and communicated the worth of their entire team

The point is, are we doing our due diligence to ensure we're respecting the industry and each other with a true understanding of what we're able to accomplish in our body of work? Our commitment should be genuine, not predicated on whether others expect or even fully understand the line we uphold. It's our duty! If you're wondering how to set the record straight with a manager/interviewer, don't worry, you'll soon see how I handle that.

Marketing Coordinator does not equal Account Coordinator

During my stumbling process—I'll stick with that phrase as it's much more realistic than churning it up to sound like some graceful ascent to becoming a marketing director. Part of the 50-plus jobs I applied for throughout the years, along with the 20 face-to-face interviews, I encountered what I call the "no differentiation interchange."

The company was a tech startup that had recently landed a major government contract. According to the job description, they were looking to hire their very first Marketing Coordinator. Sweet! At this point, I had close to six years of marketing experience under my belt and was already halfway through a master's in marketing. I could totally do this! So, I applied and received an offer letter two interviews later.

Have you ever been demoted before you even started a job? I have! Ouch!

I applied and interviewed for a Marketing Coordinator position; the offer was for an Account Coordinator, a position I had not even applied or interviewed for. After combing through the letter, I did what any professional would do. I organized my thoughts and countered with what I considered a very respectful response.

That's not how it was received. Immediately upon receipt of my counteroffer, the CEO called me. Mind you, during the hiring process, he was laid-back, even jolly, posing softball questions like, "What's your spirit animal?" and "What makes you so passionate about marketing?" On the other end of the line, he was now exhibiting the complete opposite. Salty and slightly annoyed, he couldn't understand why I prevented his company's ability to gain extra federal funding for hiring someone in a "rural community" zone to co-lead a startup marketing department while holding an entry-level title.

"Well, sir, I applied for a Marketing Coordinator position. That's the compensation and title I expect if I choose to work with you." Then, reminding me of his status as a career engineer, he said there's no differentiation between types or levels of engineers. So, it was unreasonable for me to contend a differentiation in levels of marketers.

First of all… what? A quick Google search debunked his first theory.

Second of all, how dare you!

It's a major red flag if anyone in any organization brushes off, belittles, or becomes verbally or visibly frustrated over the mindful protection of your career path in an industry in which you are a trained professional. At this point in my career, accepting an entry-level position meant it would take me years to build back to where I was currently qualified to enter. I get it, though; he wasn't a marketing expert. Rarely, those responsible for hiring marketers are, and that's why we're needed in the first place. This is an opportunity to begin the education process if we're going to be respected as industry leaders.

If you're thinking, "Well Sarah, I'm happy you can afford to turn down a job to educate an employer about marketing. I'm just not in that position."

Don't worry; I wasn't either!

Our family was less than two years into completely starting life over again after leaving a 16-year military career. At this time, we were mainly living off my husband's 401(K), along with a few marketing consulting clients. Our kids were on medical welfare with just barely enough coming in to cover our living expenses. But, with a depleting 401(K), those days were quickly coming to an end.

So, the question was, "How long will I have to take two steps back before getting to move one step forward?" Only you can answer that question. For me, this was NOT about to be that point in my career. I still had some time as I neared the completion of my master's, and I was aiming for something better and less sales-y. I was not ready to bend on this. A ridiculous battle, maybe, but I needed to stand my ground for the sake of the industry and my self-respect. At this point, our life situation had nearly stripped me of that, and I wasn't about to let this guy peel it back one centimeter more.

"No, sir. My knowledge and expertise are worth more than the entry-level title and the $18,000 a year you're offering. I wish you all the best with your search. Goodbye."

That experience was a tough lesson in protecting my craft. But as an industry, do we know how to back our professional expertise and stand by what we know to be true?

With 91% of marketers seeking out rudimentary guidance on "What are the best ways to engage my audience?"—a question that marketers should be able to fully answer with less than three years' experience—I'm afraid the industry isn't quite ready to uphold the global respect it deserves. Just nine ticks away from 100% of marketers have to ask this question illuminates major inherent flaws weakening the industry's integrity.

Defining Roles

As a realist, I'm well aware that it takes time to tackle this topic fully. Heck, when I had less than a year in the industry, I struggled with it. But a year after stepping into a new role—in a new industry—a good marketer should possess the skills to get to the bottom of that question. Instead, marketers are in roles for years, still trying to figure out how to engage their audience. Unacceptable.

Employers and clients should expect that their marketer(s) know how to best engage their audience. And why don't they? It's most likely the result of assigning marketing tasks to the youngest employees because "they understand that stuff better." This reason is another solid contender for why when organizational leaders sit down at the hiring table, there's no differentiation between Marketing Managers and Account Coordinators.

Defining the most common focus areas in marketing, along with a list of job titles frequently associated with each, will get you off to a good start:

General Marketing: Typically titled the CMO or Director of Marketing, this role is on the senior leadership team and responsible for hiring, creating and managing an overall strategy. Additionally, they ensure that technical skills are embodied and deployed by all the following roles.

Brand Marketing: Typically titled the Brand Manager or Strategist, this role maintains the brand's identity by working closely with the CMO on all messaging.

Content Marketing: Typically titled the Content Marketing Manager, this role works with the brand and content teams on a daily basis to build and manage an editorial calendar that delivers content aligned with the company's goals and objectives. This is the bridge between the sales team and senior marketing staff.

Digital Marketing: Typically titled the Director of Digital Marketing, this role crafts digital marketing strategies, designs content to fit each digital channel, and constantly monitors the analytics to measure the efficacy of each campaign. Deploys messaging created by the content marketing team as part of the strategy developed between the CMO, Brand Manager, and Content Manager.

Email Marketing: Typically titled the Director of Email Marketing, responsible for establishing an ongoing email relationship between the company and its audience. Email marketers work cross-functionally with the entire marketing team to ensure that the email strategy is consistent with the organization's overall messaging goals.

Marketing Communications: Typically titled the Director of Communications, this role is the voice of the company working with designers, writers, and digital marketers to research the audience and create engaging pitches, compile analyst briefings, update their CRM, or talk with advertisers and the press.

Market Research: Typically titled the Market Research Analyst, this role provides insights to the whole team about how to position the right products at the right price to the customers who need them. They plan, design, and implement research campaigns, using tools like user interviews, data analytics, and focus groups to gather quantitative and qualitative information.

Partner Marketing: Typically titled the Director of Influencer Marketing, this role looks for collaborative opportunities to promote with partners to their mutual benefit. Partnerships allow brands to access new audiences, ideally offering a more complete customer experience together than either would separately.

Product Marketing: Typically titled the Director of Product Marketing, this role is typically a cross-over from the sales team who are both market and product experts. The product marketing manager's job is to ensure that the market understands the value of the company's product and drives customer demand and product adoption.

Social Media Marketing: Typically titled the Social Media or Community Manager, this role understands the nuances of every major social media platform and how to adapt content messaging for each. They need to be numbers-savvy, work with data analytics tools to understand the audience and real-time measurements of social activities, and articulate how social media impacts the messaging pieces of the overall strategy.

For the sake of technical concepts, marketing has not changed—just expanded. What has changed are the tools we use and the voice and platforms in which we share our message. For that reason, when folks claim they have your "next best marketing solution" without easily defined and clearly substantiated results, reasoning, or resolution ... run!

Description of a True Marketer

A good marketer shows what their work can do, has proven case studies, un-skewed statistical facts, and analytical breakdowns. They can simplify even the most difficult marketing concepts, furnish testimonials based on tangible accomplishments, and clearly define the difference in marketing roles within an agency. This allows the organizations they work with to better understand the value they're paying for and how to optimize consumer-driven growth. That's our job as marketers, not merely filling a position for the sake of pay. That's the definition of a job, not a career.

Marketers Don't Know How to Market

Another leading question 89% of marketers asked within the last decade—relating to a foundational skill a marketer must master—"What are the best social media marketing strategies to use?" Again, revealed in the "2020 Social Media Examiner Report," WAY too many marketers are scrambling for an answer that they would've discovered within the first few years of their advanced education journey. While the majority of this group concedes that 86% of social traffic results in increased exposure, 78% increased web traffic, and 67% higher results in lead generation, they still don't understand how to engage their audience to realize these goals during the content creation process. That means that roughly 90% of marketers are struggling with the most basic of skills. If I were a betting gal, I would put all my money on this very issue contributing to the root of the problems plaguing the marketing industry.

What it comes down to is, statistically speaking, marketers don't know how to be marketers!

Could a doctor, lawyer, veterinarian, or sports star get away with this margin of error in their professions and still be respected? I think not! If we aren't operating as subject matter experts, we can't go around claiming that title. But that's what way too many marketers are doing. With roughly 90% of polled marketers not understanding how to operate in and measure two of the most basic marketing skills, it's clear marketers think much higher of themselves than they can actually prove. People in marketing roles talk about strategy and platforms, but what are the quantifiable results being articulated to leadership?

Strategies aren't a shot in the dark; they're a plan of action that results in achieving a key performance indicator (KPI). If we can't prove the results we're paid to achieve, how will others respect it, much less value it amid the next economic downturn? Which now seems to be hot on our heels. It's not just about logos, funnels, and click-throughs; it's about establishing an initial touchpoint to enter a long-term and clearly defined relationship with a very specific audience. Besides, marketing is the use of a masterful mix of communication outlets based on where your customers are.

Why Social Media Marketing Isn't Working For You

It becomes obvious why much of what is sold as marketing these days is nothing more than smoke and mirrors. Don't even get me started with pay-per-click advertising! Pahleeese! I'm not saying it isn't a useful tool, but our industry continues to be inundated with shiny one-and-done solutions that are just a single piece of the whole puzzle. In reality, we end up glorifying the end pieces and never realize the whole picture. The same applies to social media marketing. If you're focused on social only, you're neglecting pivotal puzzle pieces that complete the whole marketing landscape.

In contrast, I've learned and practiced an exhaustive marketing mix required to maintain an average 60% organic engagement rate across social media, resulting in heightened overall brand awareness. Want to know how much I spent on digital ads the year I discovered that little ditty? $75! And I'm honestly wondering why I even spent that. Part of the testing process, I suppose. But, it certainly had no bearing on reaching such brag-worthy performance levels. You know where I spent the bulk of my ad dollars during the deployment of this strategic mix? In video production, print and on the radio.

There's a very popular radio show that spans regional listenership. Knowing this show holds the attention of thousands of interested outdoor explorers, I ran a month-long giveaway commercial directing listeners to sign up on a specific website URL landing page. During that same month, I focused social media content efforts on showcasing our outdoors with stunning video and photography to accompany the audience-specific radio ad. As potential visitors navigated to our website, they began following us on their preferred social channel.

By interweaving a consistent message online and off, the mix expanded communications well beyond the radio. During that same month, we saw a 200% increase in web traffic and wound up with 190 new email subscribers, and increased our social engagement by 20%. Doing the initial work to earn new potential customers has, in turn, resulted in increased visitation to our Northeast Alabama county in the past year.

Here's the thing: I haven't accomplished anything that outlandish. I accomplished this by being a good marketer, deploying basic skills, and properly positioning the organization in front of the right audience as any professional should. These are benchmarks that all marketers can achieve. If marketers don't know how to reach and maintain this level without solely relying on paid advertising, we need to address inherent technical flaws.

To those functioning as marketers and working in the marketing field, if your work results do not lead to increased organic reach, you require more training and experience.

The "2020 Social Media Marketing Industry Report" reveals that 86% of marketers indicated that their social media efforts generated more exposure for their businesses, with 78% reporting positive increased traffic results. But still, we see overall declining social media benefits since the 2019 report was released:

- Increased exposure fell to 86% from 93%.

- Increased traffic declined to 78% from 87%.

- Generated leads lowered to 67% from 74%.

- Developed loyal fans shrunk to 60% from 71%.

- Improved sales plummeted to 59% from 72%.

- Grew business partnerships dropped to 49% from 56%.

- Provided marketplace insight fell to 49% from 58%.

- Increased thought leadership declined to 46% from 56%.

2020 Social Media Marketing SocialMediaExaminer.com
Page 7 of 46 Industry Report © 2020 Social Media Examiner

Are you even marketing?

If we all know marketing works, including but not limited to social media, and have the statistical data to back it up, why are we still hearing things like, "I don't need a website; I have a Facebook page?" Or, "I wish social marketing worked for me. I've tried, and it doesn't." Or even the dreaded, "Print is dead!" No, it's not!

I always like to do my research, so upon visiting said social pages of folks posing this question, I usually find that it's packed with a multitude of sales messaging lasting two, maybe three weeks, followed by three-plus months of little to no content at all. Until the next sale or "big announcement," where the cycle repeats itself over again a few times a year.

You tried?

No, you did not try! Instead, you stuffed a sales message down the throats of your 425 followers, of which less than 1% saw due to historically sporadic social activity (the algorithms and your customers are fed by consistency) before you made the decisive and very public proclamation that social marketing didn't work for you.

Fun fact: If you haven't posted on social media within weeks, never mind months, millennials question whether you're even in business any longer. If they happen to stumble upon your social profile during your content slump, forget about converting them to anything more than someone who once visited your page.

The industry problems are mounting. Too many marketers don't know how to engage their audience, aren't aware of how to create and stack content for results, don't know how to reverse-engineer marketing mishaps, then reshape and correct the course. As a result, they struggle to engage an audience organically or build trackable strategies that lead to results. To their detriment, they rely on paid media for views and don't listen to customer needs, get blinded by shiny new tech—thinking that new marketing is better marketing—while prematurely calling themselves experts. As a result, we're starting to see a decline in consumer trust, messaging potency and marketing efficacy.

The hard truth is there are way too many wannabe marketers, and they're making hard-working marketers trying to maintain the purity of our craft look bad!

Unfortunately, this is the reality that career marketers have to contend with while righting the wrongs left in the wake of poor marketers and potential employers such as Mr. "No Differentiation" Engineer.

So, if everyone is really a marketer, why do the numbers reflect a struggle in providing effective performance results? Although many have the potential, we need to ask whether the industry as a whole is good at marketing. The answer is not right now, and what are you as a marketer going to do about it?

To the marketer who puts their heart, soul, and even their sleep into perfecting your craft and moving the industry forward — I would like to personally hear from you to offer you my sincerest thanks. Oh, and selfishly I'd love to have someone to geek out with! You know better than anyone how hard it is to find someone else who speaks our language, let alone listen without eyes glazing over within 2.75 seconds. This is for you! Find me at @MRSDSTAHL on Instagram.

NOTES

Chapter 3

EDUCATION AND EXPERIENCE

If you live with someone younger than twenty-one, you know a thing or two about how the up-and-coming generation considers investing in higher education. To go to college or not go to college. It's like watching a nerve-wracking love story play out in real-time. When my teen talks about it, she speaks about how to do what she loves but still take wise steps toward a profitable profession. Of course, I answer with, "My dear, one thing you will never do in this life is die of boredom."

Think about it. In life, we are forever learning, whether it be through the education process or by experience. When you fill your life with a balance of both, you'll never go wrong because you'll never stop growing. Knowing we never really "arrive" hopefully, we just deepen in knowledge and understanding. Of course, some folks have more experience than education and vice-versa. With the way generational minds are shifting, for marketers, the balance lies somewhere between an equal reliance on both. Those heading toward a marketing career are trying to figure out what that lifelong balance looks like as early as 15.

I don't necessarily consider formal education the end-all-be-all, just as I don't consider real-world experience the single solution to becoming a trained marketer. Education provides the foundational technical training to pull from an experiential tool belt when necessary. It also provides the wisdom and confidence in an area of expertise that you'll most likely one day soon master!

Real-world experience allows for better comprehension of practical applications rooted in nuances that formal training can't even touch. Together, marketing education and hands-on experience fill one another's gaps, placing you in a well-rounded position that you can't achieve by taking only one path. I discovered this truth while stumbling along my own professional route, and I'm so glad I did! You'll see how education and experience went hand-in-hand to catapult my capabilities to impact businesses in significant and quantifiable ways.

Marketing Confusion

Marketers, here's a scenario you may be awkwardly familiar with. You show up at your new organization and discover every employee—and maybe even their cousin—can post on the company's social media platforms. Any old thing at any old time. In this circumstance, the first task for a marketer is evaluating who is qualified to operate in those roles and then develop a communication strategy that must now be enforced—by you. As a new employee, it's a difficult situation. However, a well-trained marketer understands how to navigate the situation and play clean-up before the real work even gets started.

Now, to the employers who allow the above scenario to unfold, um, no, it does not "help add variety and keep your employees creative." Nor does it make sense to let your youngest employee monitor your web presence because "that generation knows how to navigate that stuff better." Relationship to management, age, proximity to a computer, or just plain old curiosity does not a good marketer make.

Want to hear something even crazier? That *is* the setup in many organizations where their "marketers" are hired or placed in positions with very little understanding or expectation of the tasks necessary to market right.

Why in the world would we—as innovative professionals—think that marketing management is not a worthy enough position to be filled by the most experienced, educated, and seasoned professionals possible? Because business marketing culture is too confused over what makes a good marketer and what each role in the department plays. Why? Because, at some point, marketers lost their ability to be master connectors, storytellers, communicators, and analyzers. Therefore, a craft that should be thriving for any business in any market is not.

Why Higher Education?

One of the top questions potential marketers ask me is, "Do I really need to pursue higher education, or can I just learn marketing myself?" The simple answer is yes, to both! But the complex version of this solution is never simple. Knowing my answer will affect a major life decision that costs time, money, and valuable resources, all I can offer is my most honest thoughts based on the experience I've gained over the past ten years.

I'm a mother of three who understands all the loopholes, shortcuts and hacks to keep the grocery bill for a family of five under $200 a week. So, my answer to that question is seen through the same realistic lens. There are ways to spend less on education while getting the most out of it. There are also ways to gain experience without relying totally on the opinions of someone who never worked a day in the industry. While the workforce continues to shift for every career, in my opinion, the marketing field still requires an equal balance of education and experience. For that reason, I believe it's vitally important to develop the two in parallel to one another.

Sharp-Shooting, Etsy, and Kids

I joined the Army at 18, fell in love with an Airforce guy at 20, and started a family together by the whopping age of 21. After experiencing deployment, I didn't want to put myself in a situation that meant leaving my brand-new baby behind, so I chose to part ways with the military after three years of active duty service. Overnight, I went from a world-traveling, Humvee-driving, sharp-shooting finance specialist to a stay-at-home military spouse who managed our growing household. A major shift for a gal whose childhood dream included owning a bed and breakfast and drinking coffee on the porch with my German Shepherd. I found myself in a wildly different reality.

Although things turned out a tad different than I had imagined, I was totally okay with that. Shortly after our son came along, with two little ones under three, I learned something quite surprising for a new parent. Kids go to bed early! Just past the nursing phase, our kids went to bed regularly by 7 pm.

Still, in my early twenties, I wasn't even close to being tired before 10 pm. While trying to explain my restless heart and mind to my husband, he recommended taking up a hobby. A hobby? I never considered doing something just to pass the time. I needed to be productive! So, the next time I wrangled up the littles for storytime at the library, I snuck over to the hobby section and happened upon a book on paper crafting, of all things.

Lessons From Wedding Invitations

Back at the reading circle, a fellow mom noticed my book and told me about her sister's thriving crafting business on Etsy. This was 2007, shortly after Etsy had launched, and nowhere near the maker's movement of today. So that night, after

7, I sat down with my paper crafting book and checked out Etsy for the very first time. I was fascinated by sellers who possessed every handmade skill imaginable were actually making money as they launched their business on the world's first social selling "makers market" channel. Yup, this is where I belonged; I could just feel it.

I had stumbled on a neat project and began to pursue a paper crafting hobby that I secretly planned to turn into a thriving business. I started with greeting cards, then moved into matching sets and a myriad of monogram customizations when I finally landed on a custom wedding invitation opportunity. Not just any invitation. I'm talking three-fold fanciful delicacies that required me to know every detail of a bride's wedding plans long before her guests knew what was coming.

I coordinated design requests, took orders, communicated information, procured designer paper, cut, printed, and constructed while my well-wishing husband tied more silk bows than he will ever admit to. I was pretty pleased with my growth during year one, then things got interesting. Etsy had a social section built into the website called, Alchemy. It was a place for users to start conversations on anything that interested them. Folks connected around pretty much everything from "Meet other crafting moms in Kansas" to "Where can I find someone to turn my grandmother's dress into a bear for my daughter?" If there was a craft-related interest to be had, there was a conversation happening about it. So that's where I went when a special bride request came in for me to make a customized World of Warcraft wedding invitation set. A what now?!

Sure. I can figure this out... I think. The worst that can happen is I'll have to tell this bride that I can't pull it off, so why not at least ask and see what Alchemy can do for me? I punched my question into the conversation thread, and a digital designer from Springfield, Massachusetts, answered the call. Not only was she close to where I was from and a gamer herself, but her artistic abilities rivaled anyone I've ever seen. On top of that, she offered to customize the set for the bride at a reasonable price. Sold. That was in 2008.

Merrilee and I made many beautiful things together! But crafting digital designs on paper was just the beginning. Our love for business sparked a close friendship, and she became part of every conversation I had about bettering the business and taking it to the next level. Taking in more and more custom invitation orders on paper, I should have been a lot more successful. Instead, I was just breaking even.

Self-Employed and Making Connections

At this point, I connected with others in the industry who could help me solve some of my most pressing paper problems. My paper supplier, at the time, had a map on their website that showed where other customers who brokered their products were located throughout the country. Wouldn't you know, they had one other customer in Alabama, and that customer lived exactly where we were stationed at the time, Montgomery. What a coincidence! I had to call her! We had to be friends! Before I even heard her voice, I was determined to partner up and do anything I could to help her. Temisha answered the phone, and I'm so glad she did! To this day, although our focus has shifted, we still help each other in business, and she's even the author of this book's Forward.

What started as a grassroots goal to get better in the paper business launched a marketing career once I decided to finalize an undergrad degree. While earning a Bachelor of Business, I was shocked at how little attention was put on marketing or understanding the customer, one of the main reasons I sought higher education in the first place.

After being in business for myself for several years and seeking answers to tip the scales of operating in the red, I graduated wanting more than I'd gotten out of it. Deciding to pursue specified higher education turned out to be a necessary step responsible for some of my most incredible professional breakthroughs. I continued practicing in my business and seeking answers to all of my endless questions. Like, why do some customers respond to social posts while others don't? Or, why do some customers open emails and others don't? And, what is the best way to ensure I'm in front of the right customer?

I discussed it all with Merrilee as we continued to work together to find creative ways to take things to the next level. At some point, we realized we outgrew paper and longed for something more. Now 2013, I graduated from Faulkner University when my passion for marketing finally surpassed my passion for paper. At that time, our conversations began to shift heavily around the topic of brand building, digital marketing, web development, and how to measure its effectiveness. That's when I started dabbling in web development as we saw a need emerging in the business community. There was a need to build a presence not entirely reliant on the reach of a social platform: website building! Another skill Merrilee had mastered.

Due to our close friendship, she spent hours teaching me and patiently assisting me as I stumbled through the nuances of WordPress for months on end. Of course, the long discussions about how colors affect customer moods and how palette combinations speak a sub-conscience language seemed boring to others. We could talk or argue (we did that too) for weeks on end. We'd become best friends and business partners before we knew it.

Thankfully, I picked up my first marketing client within weeks of graduation. Now, Merrilee and I had our very first real-world opportunity to leverage the experience of our combined skills to elevate a business's brand and marketability. The shift came naturally, so we went with it.

As I built up a clientele, I consulted Merrilee on everything. I hired her to complete design pieces that I couldn't physically deliver on in the brand and marketing packages that I sold. Throughout, we maintained a grounded touchpoint with Temisha as her unrivaled savvy for business development kept our feet on the ground. If we were the dreamers and doers, she was the brains!

The Question That Changed Everything

First up was INCARE Technologies, and the gentleman who connected me with their CEO was our son's piano teacher. One day, at the end of a lesson, we got into a marketing discussion debating the importance of having a presence on social media and how cross-platform brand messaging affected customer acquisition. At the time, I didn't know the company he worked for had $15,000 earmarked for a radio campaign but were in the market to consider something a little riskier. Trust me, in 2013, it was risky to hire a contract marketing coordinator to build and maintain a socially web-based brand presence. So, big props to him for having the vision and guts to consider it.

During our initial call with INCARE senior staff members, the CEO asked me the single best question he could have ever asked. It's the question that set my career trajectory on a course I could not have foreseen, and for that, I thank him! He said, **"What's the return on investment (ROI) for our six-month social commitment?"** My first reaction was bewilderment. Dumbfounded, I thought, "There ain't no way he asked the radio people this question!" But luckily, we were on a call, and he couldn't see me squirming. Competing for my very first contract, you better believe those were NOT the words that came out of my mouth. "That's a great question, sir, one I plan to get to the bottom of for you if you're willing to give me a chance."

Long before I was even awarded the contract, I started researching "How to determine social media ROI." At the time, I listened to every *Social Media Examiner* podcast, read books and blogs, and watched YouTube videos.

Guess what I figured out?

There wasn't a single marketing "expert" that could answer that question in 2013.

That had to change. To my delight, INCARE placed that $15,000 bet on me, and I didn't want my first shot in my new field to be a disappointing one. Not for my first client, not for my future customers, and certainly not for our budding business.

During my initial social ROI research process, I discovered some deeper secrets within Google's free analytical tools. For this particular client, I learned to set up goals in Google Analytics to track every lead conversion that filtered through their website. "Lead conversion" is a trackable action that someone takes on your website, set up by you, based on your organization's marketing goals and/or Key Performance Indicators (KPIs), whether that be tracking a page count visit, time on the site, a form completion, or a purchase. Those parameters are set based on a trackable key that monitors the health of your brand's messaging path from holistic online performances.

Since the CEO had clearly expressed the importance of gathering leads through their newly updated website, it was important to focus on a creative yet powerful format to prompt leads that resulted in their niche target market taking action. So, I started with the low-hanging fruit — a giveaway, of course, back when it did not violate Facebook's Community Guidelines to host a newsfeed contest. IN-CARE(K12) was a company branch that provided the infrastructure ability for a one-to-one classroom setting. The end-users of the infrastructure they built were teachers and students. So, I got to work getting to understand the technical connectivity problems their end-users currently faced in the classroom. Without knowing the pain points of the end-user, I'd have never learned how to communicate with them, let alone convert them as customers.

Real-World Answers

Connecting directly with the end-user, we launched a video contest to win a free tech-based setup in the classroom. The winning school's video submission would be hosted on the newly re-organized website. This would show connectivity between the company's impact in their community while using it as a tool to inspire visitors to take action based on users that shared the same problem and solution. I even went as far as using it as part of a catchy call to action found in their website's footer. It's since been removed, but you can still watch the winning video submitted by Lawrence County High School in Moulton, Alabama on YouTube: https://youtu.be/ApFhcRwjP00

I leveraged user-generated content to engage their ideal customers long before it was even a catchphrase. Creative customer connection ideas come naturally to marketers seeking to serve customers regardless of era. This was a practice that came about simply by putting the customer's need first within a month of starting the contract. Social ROI, here we come!

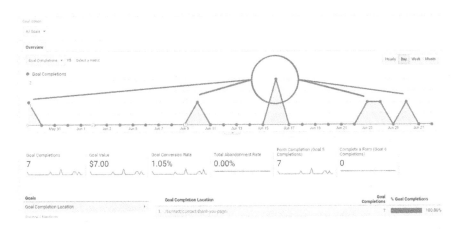

Taking it a step further. I used the community-led content to generate leads and track web form inquiry conversions. The above spikes represent the tracking initiation each time a visitor filled out the main call to action, which I set up. A goal is when a visitor completes the desired task on your site. In this case, the main call to action was form completion. I accomplished this by:

1. Setting up a Goal in the Google Analytics dashboard.

2. Tracking each step that led to the conversion.

3. Used the results to make specified content and precise marketing decisions.

Something I had not learned in school yet, the results allowed me to track the path of each lead obtained through the website. Allowing the sales team to engage one-on-one with each educator who inquired.

Short Tail vs. Long Tail Keywords

This spike represents the long tail keywords typed into Google search that resulted in a tracked form completion. What's the difference? Short tail keywords are more general search queries consisting of a few words like "restaurants near me." While long tail keywords consist of entire sentences like, "What is the most popular restaurant in Scottsboro, Alabama?"

When looking for keyword suggestions, novice marketers are tempted to focus solely on short tail keywords since these terms often yield the most traffic. However, **the long tail helps experienced marketers better understand what's going on in the searcher's mind, allowing us to adjust messaging to speak directly to solutions for customer pain points**. This reveals a niche market conversation that is much easier to break into—because the conversation sources and traffic competition are thinner—presenting an opportunity to dominate the niche conversation and stand out among competitors.

The "goal tracking tool" in Google Analytics differentiates where traffic originated and is a significant aid in determining social media return on investment. In fact, long tail keywords receive more organic recognition in Google search than the more traditional one to two high-performing word pairs.

The article "Long Tail Keywords: Win at SEO and Acquire More Qualified Leads," found on the *Business 2 Business* website, further explains how this keyword trend is getting more play and resulting in relevant conversions.

As the above report reveals, the collection of keywords represents what was literally typed into Google by those who found and visited the site organically. Those keywords informed blog topics that addressed problems their niche target audience faced while feeding the SEO-seeking Google monster. That was a vital step in building this client as a respected industry leader in the eyes of potential customers, which resulted in eight solid leads for the sales department to pursue during the six months we worked together. It may not sound like much, but with packages in the ballpark of a quarter million, I consider eight solid leads a fairly commendable accomplishment during the six-month contract.

All in all, I was pretty proud of what I was able to accomplish for my very first client with less than two years of trained marketing experience accompanied by roughly four years of real-world work.

At the end of six months, we ended the contract on good terms. Although to this day, I have no idea if the CEO felt his question was ever answered to his satisfaction. However, I was grateful for the opportunity to document another process, and I walked away with a better understanding that marketers must prove their results and facilitate tangible actions.

Graduate Certification

Within weeks of my contract ending with INCARE, the military moved us to our fourth duty station in Wichita, Kansas. Starting over again, I decided to use the downtime to find answers to more unanswered questions that I was struggling with.

I wanted something more concrete, connections to gaps that I continued to encounter in my work. Besides, I still hadn't completely cracked the social ROI code.

After nearly a year of exhausting online resources—I discovered the University of Florida's Master of Arts in Mass Communications. Not only was the school on the top-ten list of best colleges in America, but they focused on core communication concepts that included, you guessed it—an analytical approach on how to determine social media ROI. Even better, their master's certification consisted of only four classes and addressed each of my core questions in the syllabus. Okay, that sold me!

Answering the ROI Question

From August 2014 to March 2015, I attended the University of Florida's online graduate-level certificate course in Mass Communication and Social Media Marketing. This program enabled me to keep my future options open and diverse. If I've learned one thing in life, it's that you never know how life will play out, and it's important to be well-rounded in the area you're most drawn to and passionate about. Here, gaps in my ROI understanding finally started to close. While I expected Analytics would be my favorite class, it surprised me when Mass Communication Theory completely captivated me.

The course presented the psychological roles that the history of cultural media plays on consumer behavior and how to navigate and, in some cases, circumvent its effects. I hadn't yet stumbled onto this concept during all the self-education I pursued. But this very topic was crucial to answering the question, "How do I determine social ROI?" Not only that, but the material in that course was a core catalyst to becoming a better marketer. I applied concepts to marketing contracts that continue to maintain relevancy almost eight years later.

Math vs. People

Here is where it finally clicked for me, but first, let's set the stage.

Determining ROI is a math problem. Therefore, you must use math to find an answer. But social media is made up of people, and people are not math. So, a mathematical equation alone cannot determine why someone chose to take action with your organization. Frankly, I don't ever want math to be the complete answer.

People aren't robots, and their buying habits should never be reduced to math alone. If you're in the business of solving a problem for your customer, relying on mind-reading math solely is selfishly motivated and doesn't benefit your customer. There are much better, more ethical marketing practices that we'll soon discuss.

Consider what's happening in the privacy and cybersecurity sectors. As marketers, we have plenty of tools at our disposal without becoming so granular that we invade a customer's personal space—whether online or off. In fact, overreaching online privacy is hitting critical mass right now. In the modern marketplace, people are fighting to protect their privacy rather than openly offering up more information for the sake of market research. The public data currently at our disposal can determine a more accurate ROI than we were able to 20 years ago.

So, why isn't that enough?

It's enough for me. I'm perfectly content dealing only with the math portions that consumers are currently comfortable sharing to determine social ROI. However, please know it only reveals half the picture. Considering the psychology of it—my favorite side, the part I fell in love with during class—will always remain mathematically elusive. The good news is, the more we engage with and adjust content creation based on users' positive and negative interactions, the more we get to know our customers and better understand how to serve them. It's how I maintain over 50% organic engagement rates—something math didn't help me accomplish. And it's the answer to the question roughly 90% of marketers are trying to determine: "How do I better engage my audience?"

Understanding analytics, my listening ear, empathy for others, and ultimately my gut feelings drive such a successful content creation process. Therefore, I see no reason to change a thing about my process for the sake of a few more customers. If I'm serving people, actual humans, in ways that provide them value and benefit—the customers will come. I've already proven my ability to accomplish that.

It's a marketer's job to create human connections between the brand and customers and then develop a clear line of communication that results in a long-lasting relationship.

That is all.

New Customer vs. Retention

Did you know that it costs five times as much to attract a new customer than to keep an existing one? In marketing, the priority is to retain customers and build a loyal relationship with them, thereby avoiding back-breaking profit-sucking customer acquisition costs. This cardinal rule of business is why marketing exists and why I keep saying things like, "Marketing is the only profession responsible for managing growth across every major industry on the planet." What other department in your organization has a sole mission to maintain the most sacred touchpoints between your customer base and increased business? Then why in the world are they among the first to go when things get rough?

Putting confusion to rest once and for all, your sales department is more focused on new customers than maintaining existing ones, which is costing you **five times more**. What if you saved half of that, paid a good marketer, and retained more satisfied customers? Financially, you'd most likely break even at the very least. But what you'll gain in spades is customer loyalty, brand clout, improved consumer reputation, and more positive word-of-mouth referrals. So do you think it's worth keeping marketing around a little longer now? To me, it's simply a better business decision.

Now, for those who like math, let's look at the math.

Your customer acquisition cost (CAC) is calculated by simply taking all total costs associated with acquiring more customers (marketing, advertising, and sales expenses) divided by the number of customers acquired in the period the money was spent.

For example, if a company spent $100 on marketing, advertising, and sales in a year and acquired 50 customers in the same year, their CAC is $2.00 per customer.

While it costs somewhere between 5 and 25 times more to acquire new customers, it costs 40% less to sell to an existing customer. Having balanced communication scales between new and existing customers is literally the difference

CUSTOMER ACQUISITION COST

$$\frac{(\text{Marketing} + \text{Advertising} + \text{Sales Expenses})}{\text{Number of Customers Acquired}} = CAC$$

between the sales and marketing departments and why the two need to partner, not compete with one another. Now, if the marketing department were to increase customer retention rates by 5%, you'd see increases in profits by 25% to 95%.

Unacceptable social media marketing behavior

If you're anything like me, you're frustrated with hearing how social media managers push businesses to have a social presence. Only to discover their platforms are managed in a way that promotes little sense of community and customer retention, producing low-performing results.

So, how do you know if the marketer you're working with is doing it right? There are a few ways to recognize best/worst practices. First, let's take a look at what's no longer acceptable social media marketing behavior.

1. **No more unplanned presence on social media**. Your marketer should have a planned strategy with an expert ability to use planning tools, build and schedule posts with several brand parameters in mind, then articulate why they adjusted the plan every month based on follower engagement.

2. **No more outsourcing social to the youngest employee or a company that is just responsible for maintaining your social presence with no overall growth or lead conversion plans**. Remember, age isn't the only factor to consider when working with a marketer. There's so much more to it, as you're beginning to see.

3. **No longer do what "everyone else" is doing on social media.** *You* are your own corporate brand, and that must be apparent in every communication touchpoint with your customer or potential customer. Don't apologize for that. You'll hear a story about them in a bit, but do you think Poopourri cares that everyone is not their customer?! Nope! They sell a bathroom deodorant spray to young women who think poop is funny! Trust me, not everyone is their "target audience," but they have built an empire selling the stuff. Later, I'll tell you how.

4. **Don't neglect to measure the results of each online action**. What will math do? It will help you calculate how your organic engagement rates im-

pact sales with your organization. This is a cardinal rule in marketing that is of utmost importance. If a marketer is not quantifying without a prompt from you, they need more training for their over-promised services.

5. **Don't make the mistake of thinking this "social thing" will go away**. Social has forever changed how consumers make purchasing decisions. So, it's critical that you understand this concept and how it applies to your future brand development in a socially connected world—no matter which platforms are currently available.

With 78% of consumers saying that a company's social media posts impact their purchase decisions in a major way, it's clear there's been a mindset reset. The only way to make a lasting impact is to learn how to use it properly. I certainly don't mean "my cousin taught me how to…" properly. I'm talking bona fide marketing executive execution here.

As an ever-evolving marketer, I'm constantly testing out new theories based on the psychology of how people use and respond to social channels. These theories have grown from both my real-world and higher education experiences.

Marketing from Ground-Zero

While we were stationed in Wichita, I earned my second through fourth clients. But the neatest experience came from what I learned while working with a local realtor to create a parallel destination marketing brand. Here, I gained experience building a social presence from scratch, using the following steps to grow their Facebook page from 0 to 1,600 fans in just 3 months and no paid ads. In 2015, this was unheard of! Heck, today it's almost unheard of because of ever-changing social rules. Unfortunately, I can no longer pull this exact scenario off due to current social regulations, but there are still ways to accomplish similar results.

The client was looking to hire some sort of Media Manager… I think. To this day, I can't remember the job title. I even had to stop and ask for clarification during the interview because the task-to-title ratio didn't add up. Upon further investigation, it became clear he was looking for some sort of (youngish) office greeter who could help with social media and lead generation, with a focus on sales. Of course!

That's when I discovered the gross misalignment of what employers think of marketers and what marketers actually do. I respectfully told him that I wasn't a good fit for the position and that my experience was outside the wheelhouse he was looking to fill. His response was quite surprising, posing a fascinating scenario.

"Sarah, I'm one who strongly believes that good positions must be created around the talent that presents itself."

Go on; I'm listening.

"I think there is a place for you—managing a project that I'm looking to build— as my business partner."

Interesting. "What would that look like?"

"As a leading area realtor, I want to break into and lead the market of folks looking to relocate to Wichita. I've already purchased the domain livewichita.com (a site now no longer available), but I'm not sure how to develop it. What if I hired you to develop it?"

Interesting. "How does $25 an hour sound, on a part-time trial basis in which I work from home two days a week?" At this point, we had three kids at home, the youngest was barely two, and I was trying to maintain family stability first and foremost with a looming deployment in the not-so-distant future.

Deal!

That's how I became Marketing Manager for a startup real-estate tool that introduced newcomers to the livability of various Wichita neighborhoods. I immediately began developing the brand from the ground up, starting with the following tasks that took three months to accomplish.

Live Wichita added 4 new photos
Posted by Sarah Stahl [?] · December 28, 2014 · ✈

The ingenuity of local entrepreneurs here in Wichita never cease to amaze me; and it's happened again with the introduction of the world's only Grand Wagoneer photo booth; right here in Wichita!

Meet Katherine and Conan, Owners of Lamphouse Photo Co. a uniquely nostalgic mobile photo booth that is changing how locals experience events; in a very fashionable way.

"We got started in this business because we wanted to bring something to Wichita that didn't exist anywhere else an... See More

4,466 people reached   279% ORGANIC REACH   Boost Post

Like · Comment · Share · 👍 51 💬 9 ↪ 13

The Great Giveaway

Initially, I conducted a competitor analysis to see how locals responded to related online content and paid close attention to what elicited responses and why. I used the information from my initial analysis to identify what caused a community-minded response. Then, I set up a contest that lasted an entire month, giving away tickets and gas cards to help locals do the things they already loved: enjoying their hometown in new and creative ways.

The contest's purpose was to grow the Facebook Page and create a buzz around four week-long contests. I ran the contests using a third-party Facebook app to capture contact information and inquire into what else they would like to "see/do" around Wichita. The results gave me a direct route to keep in touch with potential customers and offered insight into the type of content that would perform best in future posts.

Live Wichita added 4 new photos.
December 5, 2014

Meet Jamee and Christian, owners of Wichita's newest trendy coffee shop Churn & Burn located on the south intersection of Oliver and Kellogg. So much more than just a coffee shop, this place is rich in quite a few other creamy treats. Specifically their homemade ice-cream with fun flavors that include Cookie Monster and Root beer. When you enter this cozy "treatery" you are immediately met with nostalgic relics of a not too distant Wichita staple, Joyland; which makes it f... See More

7,900 people reached   493% ORGANIC REACH   Boost Post

Like · Comment · Share · 👍 83 💬 13 ↷ 49

Today, timeline giveaways are no longer acceptable according to Facebook community guidelines, resulting in your page being put in Facebook prison if you're not careful. Clearly, Facebook eventually considered this growth hack cheating. But during my Wichita project, it was perfectly acceptable marketing behavior.

With the collected information, I further discovered that there were no other private companies helping locals "rediscover" the area. Current competitors seemed to target visitors or circulate the same events everyone else was already talking about without telling the story behind them. The competitor content revealed a very shallow view of the city. I saw this as an "untouched" opportunity to give locals a fresh look at what area businesses had going on to create the foundations of a community based referral system.

While the contests continued to run, I began interviewing local business owners to build up my content calendar with stories geared towards creating a fresh perspective of the faces who made up Wichita. The microblogging narratives I composed caused some crazy responsive results and even generated three viral posts. Every one of the 1,600 new fans was from Wichita, and the viral posts happened 100% organically without help from paid ads.

A good start, but this was meant to be a tool for newcomers one day. The locally-based trust I'd established with the community was key to bringing this tool to fruition. However, due to interest conflicts and an odd workplace dynamic, I decided this was not a project I wanted to commit to further and never had the chance to see what the legs of this cold startup looked like.

Again, I walked away with great experience to show for a contract position. One key takeaway during this project—again lasting roughly six months—was that it's essential to consider your entire social presence as a campaign rather than isolated promotions.

> "Building social communities requires compelling storytelling, not awkward sales messages."

Live Wichita added 4 new photos.
December 16, 2014 ·

Meet part of the effective team of folks running The Cotillion. Their relentless dedication to preserving this retro venue, allowing thousands to enjoy stellar performances in an ageless environment, is quite remarkable. With its circular design there's no competing with "Big Heads" as you enjoy a variety of acts in this strategic setup consisting of café style seating; ensuring an enjoying view of the show from any seat in the house.
This crew takes great pride in the family... See More

3,072 people reached 192% ORGANIC REACH   Boost Post

Like · Comment · Share · 43 4 11

STILL Not Hirable!

At this point, I'm five years into my career, have a bachelor's in business administration, a master's certification in digital marketing and mass communication AND nearly five years' experience in measured marketing results while pushing the envelope of industry expectations.

Think I'm hirable?

According to the description and list published by employers, not yet and certainly not for anything substantial. I kept landing these short-term opportunities that all ended with me scratching my head. Obviously, the knowledge I gained from each was priceless, and for that, I'm not complaining.

Is this what marketing for yourself was like? A string of short-term contracts that ended before accomplishing major goals? And why six months? That seemed like the magic number where clients finally began to feel they were sinking money into a project that wasn't getting them where they wanted to be. I had three other such clients while in Wichita, working my fanny off for six months each. All with an abrupt stop because the client's perceived results were not achieved. Overall, I walked away from these experiences extremely disappointed. If so many clients were canceling contracts, disregarding the strides made within a six-month contract, what was I doing wrong? If my customers weren't happy, I had to be doing something wrong!

Do you remember when you first started your adult life? Nothing could phase you. No matter what, you felt on top of the world. Like you could accomplish anything. But year after year, you experienced disappointments, and your once vivacious candor and blatant disregard for naysayers took a backseat to reality. Then you realized that you'd become as cautious as those who once elicited your serious eye-rolling and smirks.

That was me. But rather than calling it cynicism, I'd like to think it's wisdom. Perhaps contracts ended because a clear expectation wasn't set. Perhaps I wasn't communicating well with my customers and didn't ask the right questions at the onset—and maybe I failed to pre-determine goals and didn't work in a true partnership to build in benchmarks that kept us on track. Maybe I was so eager in my work that I was going rogue on those paying.

I assumed it was all the above and began to make the necessary changes to adjust. Recognizing, articulating, and pivoting away from faults is essential for growth.

Creation of Avant Creative

At every step, I had Merrilee and constantly bounced my triumphs and failures off her. Together we continued to tweak the business and discovered something exciting while working with several of our Wichita clients. Most of the clients needed brand design and web development work. Thankfully, we had initially suspected this was the easier, low-hanging fruit sale to create a long-term customer relationship and had already done preliminary work to prepare for clients. Besides, a logo, brand kit, and website were much more tangible than digital media management can be. So, together, Merrilee, Temisha, and I pivoted to create Avant Creative—www.avant-creative.com—a full-service marketing agency "equipped to navigate the digital economy with a passion for developing measurable marketing strategies." At long last, business number two was established with a dear friend I lovingly called my number one!

"Make it so, number one!" became a phrase I often used after long conversations with Merrilee about the next steps to, once again, take it up a notch. We had a good thing going. I was boots on the ground and the face of the budding company, making contacts and converting clients. Merrilee was the creative art director, building brand pieces and coding websites, while a talented team supported our efforts. Temisha Young, who we connected with during our Paper Perfection's days on Etsy, along with expert developer and keen business insider Charles Groce. At the time, Temisha and I didn't know Charles as well, but we trusted Merrilee implicitly.

She'd tell us that we couldn't live without Charles's analytic, coding, and app development skills, so I considered him good people long before I'd have a chance to meet him in person. For a few years, the four of us worked to situate the pieces of a promising marketing agency before making a partnership official. Of course, we ran into hiccups; I mean, what group of people building something great from across the country doesn't? However, the physical distance that separated us didn't seem to keep us from trying.

Merrilee now lived in Connecticut with her beloved cats, staying up way too late watching *Battlestar Galactica* and finalizing the never-ending web development projects that were pouring in.

Temisha lived in Alabama, working in business development for the Chamber of Commerce and starting a family of her own.

Charles raised his boys back and forth between his hometown in Kentucky and development work that took him to Michigan.

Our family was deciding whether to get out of the military and take on the business full-time or not.

All of us, in our own way, faced life-altering decisions on the horizon. What could go wrong?

Deployment and Decisions

Then, the deployment caught up to us, and my husband was sent to Afghanistan just six months after arriving in Wichita; about the same time, I parted ways with the Wichita realtor. So for eight months, we were half a world apart while I managed our household, homeschooled our three kids, and built a business.

There's a cruel joke in the military that references one's number of deployments in relation to one's number of spouses. Dan and I didn't think there was anything funny about that. Married fourteen years at this point, we wanted to take our time apart seriously and do what we could to grow closer instead of apart.

A few nights before Dan deployed, we went on a date and stopped by a local bookstore to pick out a devotional that interested us both. We bought two copies and committed to read the devotion daily and stay connected through the insights the Lord shared with us during our time apart. The devotional we chose was called "Streams in the Desert." With absolutely nothing modern or New Age about it, we grew closer to the Lord and each other more than we ever imagined we could with the help of that book during the eight-month separation.

During that time, seeds were planted in our hearts to disconnect ourselves from the military. This was a decision deemed foolish by onlookers, especially with just four years remaining until a retirement that promised monthly payments and free health care—for life! But the closer we got to Dan's reenlistment date in March 2016, the clearer the decision to part ways with the military became. Finally, after much debate, prayer, and consideration, in 2016, our family decided to follow God's lead and walk away from the military, four years shy of 20 years of service. We understood the risk we were taking but felt very confident that faithful living was the only way to live.

Shortly before leaving Wichita, I was unexpectedly approached for a large-scale marketing project from a past Alabama contact. When I finished my bachelor's at Faulkner and stationed in Montgomery, we'd become quite fond of visiting the Northeast corner of the state during long weekends. Located in the foothills of the Appalachian Mountains, we held this quaint community close to our heart for many years.

So, months before separating from the military, a potential client who lived in that exact area contacted me for a long-term project. Everything seemed like it was falling into place. This opportunity allowed us to feel like we'd be okay as we transitioned into a new chapter of life.

Transitioning to Civilian Life

During the shift from military to civilian life, we thoroughly enjoyed our new-found freedom to make life whatever God was leading it to be. We were 35 and felt like we were starting life all over again, and in some ways, for the very first time. During our initial move to civilian life, we had residual military income and consistent work from two reputable clients with consistent new web and brand development projects coming in under Avant. For starting life over, we thought it couldn't be going any better. But as life would have it, we didn't quite have our happy ending.

About six months into our transition, the residual military income stopped, and one of my most valuable clients was no longer paying me for my work. To this day, the client still owes me thousands of dollars. During that time, I was working harder than ever to make the business work, and because of the rural community we landed in, my husband had no luck finding a job. Now dipping into our 401(K) to survive month after month, we felt the strain of the decision we'd made.

All I know to do in situations like that is to pray and work harder. With Merrilee's direction and encouragement, we again took things up a notch.

- I focused on speaking engagements and interviews to further solidify clout for our budding agency.

- I spoke across the region at statewide PR professional groups, with downtown business organizations, on Cliff Ravenscraft's podcast (episode 488), and for marketing classes in Huntsville and Chattanooga-based startup communities.

- For our company, I conducted a "25 days of live video" experiment in which Merrilee and I had fun talking together on Tuesdays to offer tips.

- I was actively engaged on Snapchat that led to a book contributor opportunity for Chelsea Peitz's *Talking in Pictures*.

To no avail, It seemed no matter what I did, how hard I worked, the more I participated, the less work came in. Giving up was never an option, especially after years of dedication. I remained committed to the cause even as our income opportunities began to dry up. We'd hit a wall. But I never lost hope as long as we had direction from the Lord, our family, and a great team. I was so confident in what the future had in store and refused to stop now.

Sometimes though, life leaves us in a spot that offers no other opportunity than to walk away from it all.

And Then... The Unthinkable

In 2017, the unthinkable happened. Temisha and Merrilee had been working to finalize a web development contract with the Montgomery Housing Authority. This would've been the biggest project our team landed to date. It was the project of all projects, the one that was going to finally catapult us in the growth trajectory we'd been working toward for over four years.

The day of the planning conference arrived, and Temisha was set to meet their management team in person in their Montgomery office, accompanied by a Facetime call with Merrilee. The plan was for Merrilee to answer all the technical web development questions while Temisha tackled the contractual business end of things. Temisha texted Merrilee when she arrived and gave her a ten-minute heads-up that she'd be calling soon. Merrilee replied and said she was ready to go.

Ten minutes later, and face-to-face with the clients, Temisha called Merrilee. No answer. She tried several more times, with no luck. Finally, Temisha reached a point that she had to move on with the meeting without Merrilee.

After the meeting, Temisha reached out to me to ask if I'd heard from her. I hadn't. I was alarmed because this behavior was totally unlike Merrilee, but I figured we'd get to the bottom of it soon.

No one heard from Merrilee the following day either. Since childhood, Merrilee had Type 1 diabetes, and I'd encountered similar behavior from her once before due to an imbalance. I was concerned but thought it would all be cleared up soon. When I still hadn't heard back from her, I reached out to her father. His response devastated me. The absolute worst had happened. He had gone to her apartment and found Merrilee unresponsive.

About Merrilee

Merrilee, my best friend, business partner, and closest confidante (second to my husband) had suddenly and forever left this earth. Our remaining team silently mourned our dear friend in our own way. Merrilee was an isolated touchpoint that each of us held dear. No one else in our lives knew and loved her as we did. So, no one was physically close to talk to about her, and few people around us understand the deep pain left in the wake of her passing.

But as a budding company, we had fires to fight while operating in complete and utter shock. Merrilee was the thread that held us all together, both personally and in business. Not only that, but she held the sole access to the websites we were currently building. Clients came out of the woodwork seeking access to updates, project expansions, or even simple maintenance.

The business kept us more actively engaged than we had been in months, but it was all unpaid work to gain control over the brands that Merrilee had led. That's when we quickly learned how well we all worked together. The synergy between us during a crisis and in the absence of Merrilee delightfully surprised us, and we remained hopeful that we could get through this together.

But, Merrilee was irreplaceable. She possessed skills none of us could replicate, and to this day, I have not met a single person who could fill her brand development and design role at the level of quality she was able to produce.

Wanting to honor my friend's memory, considering our current financial circumstances, I had a desire to salvage what was left of the business. But without Merrilee, it just wasn't the same. She passed just days before Thanksgiving in 2017, and by early 2018 I felt forced to find stable work. A task I knew very little about with a military and entrepreneurship background.

What do you mean unqualified?!

By the summer of 2018, I had at least 20 interviews for various marketing positions lined up, all across the Tennessee Valley region. All resulting in a similar message, "Mrs. Stahl, we found a more qualified candidate, and for that reason, we're going to take another direction," became my new normal. With dwindling income, we were running out of time and options and with no end in sight. Now, worry began to set in. The honest truth is we were growing weary of maintaining the faith that seemed to have us running on a hamster wheel. If nothing else, we learned that living a life of faith is **not** for the faint of heart.

At this point, I'd worked with Merrilee for a decade, during which the bones of a promising marketing agency emerged. During that time, we were able to:

- Develop custom websites.

- Build brands from scratch.

- Manage social accounts.

- Write copy for countless marketing materials.

- Consult on strategy from a variety of marketing and advertising angles.

Does that sound unqualified to you?

The reality set in. I was unrelatable to a system of marketing to which the industry had acclimated. Perhaps a bit ahead of my time, maybe. But unqualified? Not even a little bit.

At this point, I was starting to simply get mad.

The clarity of hindsight made it crystal clear that the decision to leave the military presented the most challenging life task my husband and I faced in our nearly two decades together. Unable to find work in Northeast Alabama, we lived on his military 401(K) for close to a year—alongside the inconsistent contract work I picked up. Our kids were on medical welfare, and all of our finances went only towards necessities to get us from one day to the next.

Master's in Marketing

My husband, clearly understanding my frustration and determination to turn our life situation around, invested in me by suggesting we take on a $10,000 loan to complete my master's. The reasoning behind that was, "Well, at least I can teach at that point, right?!" With 30 credits left to complete the degree, I decided on a master's in marketing over an MBA, mostly because colleges require more than 15 marketing credits to teach. This way, I could kill two birds with one stone. I'd have the necessary credits to teach, close the marketing gaps I maintained as a contractor, and deposit into my marketing clout bank. Something had to stick, right?

So, in November of 2017, I started a master's in marketing program with Southern New Hampshire University with a graduation date set for December 2019. If we could hold on till then, we would make it out of this. Not one to put all our eggs in one basket, I maintained my marketing contractor status along with my business partners at Avant Creative while working with clients that you can check out at Avant-Creative.com.

Tired and On the Brink

Nearing the end of 2018, I was tired.

Tired of working with very few results that translated into income for our family and tired of watching novice marketers gain positions in organizations that hurt the marketing industry's reputation.

Tired of listening to expert marketers tell businesses how to be successful and churning out very few tangible results.

Tired of being undervalued, yet somehow now being seen as underqualified. Whatever that even is.

In the late summer of 2018—on the brink of financial ruin—I was desperate for something tangible to turn up. Then, a job opening came to my attention. The title, "Director of Communications," with a Chamber of Commerce located twenty-seven miles from where we landed after leaving the military. With less than an hour commute and a reputable title, I applied. Within a week, I had a call for an interview; I was the only one of the three finalists to show up.

Salty from the path we'd been on and concerned about the position's validity—I mean, no one else showed up—I decided to lay it all out on the table during my interview.

I was not about to be confused for a sales associate or a way to test out the shiny new toy, also known as digital marketing. I may have been desperate for steady work, but I was not about to sacrifice my principles.

Surprisingly, we talked quite a bit about genuine marketing tasks. Tracking, analytics, communicating with an understood audience, and several other technical skills listed on my resume came up for the first time in my job search. Usually, the hiring manager talked more about the company and what I could do for them rather than whether my skills were a good fit for the role.

As the conversation unfolded, I dared to hope that this position was actually legit. I sat in that interview, totally conflicted over helping another organization build something from scratch or trying to make Avant work in Merrilee's absence.

Finding myself at rock bottom, what did I have to lose? I laid out an alternate plan for them to consider that would allow us to take a step forward—before knowing if it was worth the investment on both our parts. I suggested I start in a part-time capacity to see if it's a good fit. Besides, I'd already learned repeatedly that most promising opportunities last six months. Why not at least shoot for that? The initial response was, "That's not what we're looking for."

Director of Communications

To my surprise, I had an offer for that exact scenario within three days. And that's why I often say, "By default, I am now a Marketing Director for the very first time."

By 2021 I had the opportunity to run a marketing department for three years and as a result I'm firmly convinced of the following. The interplay between education and experience made it possible for me to land a Marketing Director position before 40 without working a single day in a traditional agency atmosphere—all in all, not a bad accomplishment!

The Spirit of Merrilee

I miss Merrilee something dreadful but feel confident she'd be proud and supportive of what I've accomplished in her absence. My only regret is she's not here to share it with me. The only way I know to thank her is to keep moving forward, linked through the work she did building my brand on Sarahtahl.com, using what she left behind to continue sharing her creativity, expertise, and her impact on a world left behind.

NOTES

Chapter 4

KNOW YOUR AUDIENCE

Who is your target audience?

Really, I'd like you to write down who you believe your target audience is in the notes section of this chapter. Then, when you're done with the chapter, I'm going to ask you the same question to see if you come to the same conclusion.

Your target audience is certainly much more than a list of demographic features (age, gender, and geo-location) related to income level. Think about it, does your current home address and income level wholly define who you are as a person?

Then think about this, do all people at your same income level think, act, feel, and respond to the world the same way you do?

Of course not!

But that's how many businesses and marketing professionals believe their audiences respond; thus, the billions of dollars spent addressing the pretend customer they wish they had instead of listening to true customers and adjusting to fill actual needs.

Haphazardly and with a broad sweep, assigning a group of people to an all-encompassing demographic group because, well, "the more, the merrier" is not a solid marketing approach! Besides, assuming that *everyone* is among your target market also assumes a few broad descriptors somehow make up the core psychological contributors behind purchasing decisions. How does anyone formulate a marketing strategy out of those scraps?

See what I'm getting at?

Try me. Next time you're in a marketing meeting, organically bring up the question, "Who is our target audience?" I bet that you get answers like, "At-home moms with school-age kids who love to cook and have a household income over $150k."

I hope that a marketing department can be a little more granular than "everyone who's just like us!"

First of all, no mom with school-age kids LOVES to cook! And even if she did, do you think that she's an appropriate target for both dye-free laundry detergent AND sugary breakfast cereal?

Each of those products appeals to two very different women, even if they are both at-home moms with school-aged kids who "love" to cook. Given the year of Covid, the only thing these two ladies probably have in common is that they're tired of cooking!

Customer Persona

Let's make sure we're on the same page when we talk about a target audience. As a trained marketer, finding a target audience means precisely defining what kind of people are most likely interested in and/or using your product or service. Most companies look at general demographic information. However, for customers to feel connected to a product, service, or brand, they need to relate to the content and tone of the company's message *on multiple levels*. Not just on social media! Generalized guestimations do not equal relatable messages. Crafting compelling content requires knowing intimate details about your audience.

Market research addresses your customer holistically, including demographics and psychographics that give way to a more accurate persona. When a persona emerges, so does the whole customer, including their real problems and how they're currently trying to solve them. Besides, isn't that what business is all about? Solving a problem for profit! How do you know what problem you're solving if you don't understand a specified target audience? You don't!

Personifying a target market allows an organization to develop more precise communications based on *why* clients engage in the choices they make, not just *how*. Identifying the why behind the customer purchase process offers deeper insight to help create a higher level of content creation and customer retention.

Be aware; there will be times that research doesn't include graphs, analytics, and reports. Sometimes it requires raw monitoring by listening in the right places in addition to data research reporting. There is certainly a place for it, but not always the only factor to better understand your audience. The foundation of effective content strategy relies heavily on specifying your ideal customer in great detail, revealing the best ways to communicate with them. Remember, these are **real** people.

The number-one reason businesses are overwhelmed by content creation and community engagement is because they aren't confident about who their marketing addresses.

Broad communication with customers is convoluted and confusing at the very least. What ends up happening is businesses want to try the shiny new strategy that competitors are dabbling in. Failure is inevitable because they still don't understand their community or how to precisely apply said shiny new tool for the purpose of growth.

Let me save you a lot of time and energy: Stop comparing your business to others! I implore you to spend that time learning about your customers instead. Discover who they are while finding creative and specific ways to better serve and support their needs. Let's tackle how to balance data and raw research to solve this problem.

What's Hiding in Your Data?

Following are four tools available right now that grant you access to a great deal of information about what your customers are looking for and what's most important to them. These are among the plethora of tools available to help you learn what's hiding in your data and help you narrow down your target audience. This way you'll be confident in creating content that speaks directly to them and builds your online community.

1. **Analytics platforms**: (Like Google Analytics) Offers up precise details about which website pages are currently among the most interesting to your visitors. Navigating down to the "behavior" tab and clicking on "overview" reveals your highest-performing pages.

   For instance, the top-performing post on my website while writing this book is titled — "The 70/20/10 Rule Explained in 5 Steps." Visitors spent 9 minutes on this page. That's significant reader engagement! According to *MOZ*'s study, *80% of readers never make it past the article headline, and even fewer read past the headline copy.* That means the title compelled fellow marketers to spend time learning more about this topic. Knowing the headline passed the 80% open rate test is how I learned that other marketers applied the concept to their content creation to improve connection with their audience to increase organic engagement.

Again, this aligns with the problems revealed in the annual "Social Media Examiner" report showing that a high percentage of marketers are seeking help on how to better creating content that connects customers to the brand. As a result of discovering this in my analytics, more of my content creation will be focused there.

2. **Facebook's Graph Search:** is a technical term for Facebook's platform-based search engine. Now that I know people most engaged in my best-performing post are interested in marketing, I take that knowledge to Facebook's search engine to unearth the humans behind the statistical interest. Knowing what to pursue in the search bar, I narrow my audience to specific people in my geographical location. So, I created the search topic, "people interested in marketing near Huntsville Alabama."

While I discuss privacy and ethics later in the book, this tactic is something I use for *research purposes only*. Personal details discovered on a public platform should be treated with the utmost respect, never taken advantage of or used to spam.

The goal here is to identify trends among people actively looking for the same solution your business provides while seeking opportunities to open up valuable discussions around very specific content.

Researching "people interested in marketing near Huntsville Alabama" revealed that many were interested in "The Big Marketing and PR Event" sponsored by Red Sage Communications and co-hosted by both The Catalyst and the North Alabama chapter of the Public Relations Council of Alabama. The same crowd that attended were also interested in related events, including "Strong Women, Strong Coffee," and even a class I'd previously taught, "Solutions to the Top 5 Marketing Mistakes." Additionally, many were working moms of teenagers who were active in their local band program. Finally, and to my surprise, most of the subject group were non-Alabama natives looking to plug into their new regional business community.

Within your own search, you'll find topics of discussion come to life. For example, I could write additional articles—spurring stackable social content—with titles that include "How Busy Moms Market" or "Why Moms Make Better Marketers." With a better understanding of my audience, I can create content around their interests to drive increased engagement, brand awareness, trust, and additional opportunities.

3. **Twitter's Search Tool**: Use this to identify a different side of your target audience. Available in the platform's search bar, it allows you to search a specific area of interest based on what we've discovered in previous research methods.

Starting with a hashtag, I searched #MarketingProblems, which uncovered current conversations around problems that have been revealed in a public forum setting. Presenting an opportunity for me to provide solutions. In true Twitter form, discussions vary from comical to technical and everything in between. But the beauty of this tool, in my opinion, is access to light-hearted conversations that are important to its poster.

When you engage, simply be available and authentic. That's not the time or place to amplify yourself. Instead, that's the place to reveal your humanity, connect with like-minded folks, and take the time to show you care.

Next, I adjusted my search and shortened it to "marketing in Huntsville." Here is where I found: companies, professionals, and influencers in the marketing industry located in my geographical location. In the search, you'll see a string of conversations neatly organized under one tidy topic. Here, I can choose who to follow and decide what ongoing discussions are valuable to be part of.

4. **Facebook Insights Tool (Post Performance)**: Here, you get a snapshot of the best-performing posts that generate the most engagement. However, to take your organic engagement reporting capabilities up a notch, I highly suggest using a paid customer relationship management (CRM) tool, like Agorapulse, which I discuss in another chapter. Tools like that allow you to bypass Facebook's more clunky insight tools, revealing more specific engagement data, including how you stack up against competitors.

These four free tools are just the beginning, but build well off each other during the target audience research process, and play a significant role in elevating your marketing tactics to the next level by more clearly understanding your target audience. Use these tools as a guide when conducting your research, and be sure to document your findings and use them as a guide in the content creation process.

While finding these targeted customers may seem like an overwhelming task, they're quite accessible. While advertising has become quite personalized, segmented audiences must be identified and appealed to directly in ways that resonate on an individual level. Here, I caution you to understand internet privacy rules to ensure you're not breaching consumer privacy.

Meet Maggie Markets

I get it; all that data diving can be quite daunting. So, now that you've formulated a rough sketch of your target market, let's take it a step further. Let's bring your target market to life. Starting with a name, here's where the creative process begins!

If you enjoy Pinterest, you'll love this. The reason Pinterest has roughly 300-million users is that it's a visually appealing platform with very little text and lots of awe-inspiring photos. Users compile those photos to plan out their vacations, decorate their homes, or choose a hairstyle — to help manifest the life they aspire toward. That's why I always recommend using this platform to visually bring your target customer to life.

Did you have an imaginary friend when you were a child? If you did, you know a thing or two about how to get to know and better understand someone who's there, but without physical form. All good things! Besides, imaginary friends are a symptom of developing social intelligence in children. Although companions are make-believe, children relate to imaginary beings in the same way they connect with real friends. I'm suggesting we engage in a similar social experiment as adult marketing professionals.

Meet Maggie Markets. She's come to life on a secret board under my personal Pinterest account. Based on the above information I discovered in my research process, I even assigned her a tagline: "The up-and-coming girl boss who passionately balances working and playing hard." A far cry from the at-home mom who loves to cook!

Maggie is fiercely dedicated to everything in her life: her husband, her children, her work, creating an unforgettable home life, and enjoying downtime with a very select group of close friends. Maggie is who I have in mind every time I add Maggie-approved pins and create Maggie-approved blogs. Although not visible to the public, my secret board includes infographics on how to set up an email marketing strategy, top-rated content marketing checklists, a white paper on the "16 #GirlBoss Habits Every Female Leader Should Adopt This Year," creative ideas on how to better situate and organize a workflow in your office and, of course, the best gift bag wine carriers, how to host the perfect girls' night, and top-10 vacation spots for families with teens.

See? There's so much more depth to Maggie than making lunch for her kids, dropping them off at school, and then spending eight hours behind her desk before grocery shopping for dinner. Maggie has goals. Big ones! And she's learning how to enjoy her life, balance her relationships, and take her career to the next level all at the same time.

As I sit in my office, feet propped up in my comfy chair, scrolling Pinterest, I'm conducting market research. I'm reading the #GirlBoss white paper and learning insights into making pointed connections between Maggie's goals and how I communicate with her about solving her problems in relation to my services.

Why?

As marketers, we absolutely cannot look at the "Maggie" we market to as a two-dimensional figure with lots of dollar signs floating above her avatar. That frame of reference dilutes the power of marketing down to a cold, hard sale. That's why the marketing space is so troubled today. When people who are part of the next generational shift feel the slightest iota of being JUST sold to, they will tune you out the second they sense that vibe.

We must find ways to provide appealing solutions to Maggie's pain points without interrupting her and provide opportunities of interest without creeping her out.

A thorough understanding of your target customer informs:

- who to invest time in

- who to write for

- nonprofits to align with

- magazines to advertise in

- podcasts to approach as a guest speaker

- downloadable PDF's to make available on your website

- how to time your email marketing campaign

Without fully understanding the "Maggie" in your market, how the heck have you done all that, and who were you speaking to? Acting on the one-dimensional Maggie with dollar signs hovering over her head? Stop it!

Connecting With Your Audience

A whopping 91% of marketers struggling to connect with their audience presents yet another "know your audience" issue. Don't you hate it when you're scrolling through your favorite platform and see ads that have no relevance to your life? Marketers behind those ads are plugging in the wrong targeting features, resulting in irrelevant interruption of your feed. These marketers spend their days in an erroneous mindset using hype-y tactics in their attempts to persuade, resulting in forced pattern interruption. To those marketers: Great, you're a Facebook ad whiz! Seriously, that's super-duper handy!

But if you're using it to gain traction on a look-a-like audience that skews the makeup of an authentic target audience, your wizardry is misplaced. We must know who we are speaking to and why! While a sales message cycle goes from product to purchase, a marketing message moves through several "P's" of the persuasion process. Not to be confused with the long-gone four P's of marketing—it's now been revolutionized for the modern-day, ever-evolving market ushering us into the future.

The P's of Persuasion was introduced to me by Alex Cattoni or @copyposse on Instagram during a recent Ad World conference. She's developed and mastered a six-prong pie chart approach on multiple epic marketing levels. Her "6 P's of Persuasion" cuts right through the straight-lined sales approach and applies content and messaging to a formula that builds trust, believability and inspires the right audience to take action.

Keep the following sentence in mind as you read through and develop your 6 P's:

"Customers don't buy your product; they buy the outcome of your product." ~Alex Cattoni

SIX P'S OF PERSUASION

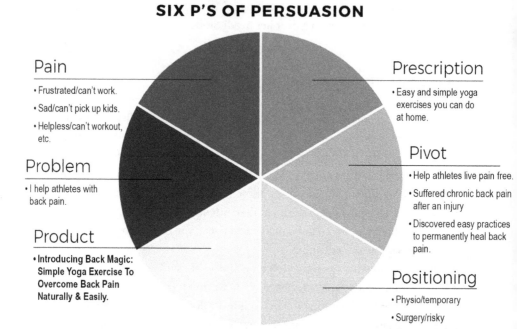

Pain
- Frustrated/can't work.
- Sad/can't pick up kids.
- Helpless/can't workout, etc.

Problem
- I help athletes with back pain.

Product
- Introducing Back Magic: Simple Yoga Exercise To Overcome Back Pain Naturally & Easily.

Prescription
- Easy and simple yoga exercises you can do at home.

Pivot
- Help athletes live pain free.
- Suffered chronic back pain after an injury
- Discovered easy practices to permanently heal back pain.

Positioning
- Physio/temporary
- Surgery/risky
- Medication/short-term

Adapted from Alex Cattoni during Ad World 2021

So, if a customer doesn't believe the product or service will help them, they won't buy it.

Problem. Articulate a clear customer problem with empathy to build trust and show that you truly understand what the customer is feeling. You are [specific pain point] because of [specific problem].

Pain. Measuring needs should feel supported, understood, heard and then articulated. You are [negative emotion/ experience/pain] because [specific problem].

Prescription. What is the solution, secret, discovery to overcome the problem? Still, no product/service revealed. To overcome [problem], you need [unique solution].

Pivot. Shift focus from them to you. Still not a focus on the product/service. Reveal your mission, reason why, or inspiration behind the solution you have created. I am on a mission to [mission] because [reason why] and I discovered [unique solution] to help [core benefit].

Positioning. Position your solution as a simpler, easier, faster way to get results. Maybe you've tried/thought of [alternative solution] but [another problem] stops you.

Product. The best, most straightforward way to overcome the problem, [insert product/service] here. The best/simplest/fastest/ easiest way to overcome [core problem] is [unique solution] that [unique positioning].

Alex's chart is a major assist when implementing proper steps to a truly persuasive marketing message that speaks directly to the pain points of a target audience.

Fill in the above blanks to propose your particular persuasive solution to the "at-home mom who loves to cook" and "work-from-home mom who hikes." Believe it or not, those are two very different women and we must be able to differentiate messaging for each, as marketers. Understanding the nuances of what makes up each is vital to nailing the content creation process at every level of marketing.

Now, who is *your* target audience?

NOTES

Chapter 5

MORE THAN ONE WAY TO MARKET: LESSONS FROM THE PIANO GUYS

Now that you realize your target audience is as multi-layered as the different types of people in the world, it follows that there's certainly more than one way to market.

To reach the depths of creative marketing, we must be well-read and well-versed on what's happening in the larger world of marketing, not just in your immediate periphery. So review marketing plans, listen to podcasts, analyze advertisements, and access breaking industry trend feeds by setting up a Google Alert and/or a Brand 24 feeds.

I set up the Google Alert "creative marketing tactics," which introduced me to The Piano Guys. Talk about inspirational insight! I'm now a huge fan of a group responsible for nothing short of a musical and marketing marvel. I mean, the things they can do with a piano and cello are enough to make even the most anti-classical music fan stop in their tracks. Their ability to convert listeners from any genre to classical-loving fanatics alone is a testament to their noteworthy marketing abilities.

I view the world through a marketing lens, so as I became a convert, I analyzed The Piano Guys' strategies and quickly realized a perfect balance of marketing tactics was responsible for their explosive growth.

A group of dads with humble beginnings went from 0 to 30 music videos that garnered 134-million views and 757,000 YouTube subscribers within their first few years of launching.

Using my analysis, I created a list called "The Seven Shocking Ways the Piano Guys will Make You a Better Marketer." These are my observations and takeaways as a marketing professional monitoring their consistent rise in mass popularity. To this day, I've had no communication with the group to confirm any of the following conclusions.

1. Evergreen Content Creation

Just like the evergreen tree, "evergreen" content is SEO (search engine optimized) content that stays continually relevant and "fresh" for readers regardless of how much time has passed. In other words, an anchor piece of content builds upon itself consistently to keep new users captivated irrespective of the initial publish date.

Remember that time *Star Wars: The Force Awakens* had the world in a delightful tizzy? Of course, you do. And during the hype, millions of people viewed The Piano Guys' epic cello battle in anticipation of the saga's newest episode.

Interestingly enough, when I dug a bit deeper, I found The Piano Guys had initially made the video four years before the new movie debut in honor of the annually recognized "May the 4th Be With You Day." Amazingly, four years later and with the world enraptured with the imminent JJ Abrams blockbuster release, the heavily ranked video had previously created the necessary standings to score a top spot in a simple "Star Wars" Google search.

Clamoring for any glimpse of the year's most-anticipated movie, new visitors quickly discovered their video, skyrocketing it to what is currently close to 30-plus million views. Then, every May 4th, the video is rediscovered and re-shared while remaining very relevant, resulting in compounding growth.

As you can see, choosing the perfect evergreen content for your company requires understanding relevancy, then using it in a way that continuously builds on a very specific branding message.

FACT: According to the *HubSpot Blog*, "*High search engine rankings are achieved because of the quality and timelessness of evergreen blog content; it will typically rank very well in search engines over time. This makes it critical for bloggers to make sure evergreen content is well-optimized with the keywords for which they're trying to rank in search engines.*"

2. Inspire others to greatness.

If you have no idea who The Piano Guys are, now that I've introduced you, be advised you'll most likely want to start playing the piano or cello immediately. Go for it! The Piano Guys made playing the cello and piano two of the most stimulating instruments on the planet, even making it easy for others to duplicate the creative compilations expressed in their epic performances. Notably, The Piano Guys don't hold their cards close to their chest. It's quite the contrary; they make it easy for other musical groups to replicate their accomplishments by selling sheet music directly from their website. At this point, you might think it strange that they expose all their best-kept secrets. The truth is, this is the catch-22 that most businesses aren't willing to risk and trail behind their competitors as a result.

FACT: Old-school tactics prohibit disclosing your secrets to your competitors, but modern marketing tactics reveal the contrary. Contributing editor Robert Craven, CEO of MegaFoods, recently wrote an article for *Entreprenuer.com* called "Let's Be Real: Why Transparency in Business Should Be the Norm." Craven revealed the key factor to building brand loyalty is through trust.

3. Delightfully entertaining.

I hope this is no longer a shock, but social media users don't actively intend to make a purchase. But they will! That's why Facebook implemented new algorithms limiting companies from viewing posts without having to pay big bucks. They are prudently trying to find the perfect mix of content (ads vs. non-ads) so users continue to stay engaged on the platform. Keeping users engaged doesn't include "buy me" posts flooding a user's newsfeed.

However, there are amazing benefits to creating content that isn't a hard sell—Facebook rewards delightfully entertaining content with organic views. Most people are on social media to unwind, relax, and typically want to be entertained. The Piano Guys have mastered this concept, a key component in their virality. Their captivating content not only stirs the soul but also includes a perfectly timed giggle here and there.

The more entertaining your content, the more free engagement you earn, which means the more you show up in the newsfeed.

FACT: "Whenever someone visits their own newsfeed, there are around 1,500 stories waiting to be seen from the people, and pages that they follow. Since the average person doesn't have the time to read through 1,500 posts, Facebook's algorithm prioritizes these stories to show users what they're most likely to be interested in based on past engagement." @ SproutSocial

4. Create an inner circle.

The Piano Guys are genuine and make their fans feel more like family than distant spectators. They credit their imaginative ideas to God, frequently shout out to fans, and encourage fellow musicians to perfect their craft. They even dedicated a complete video performance to their founders, who originally backed their wild idea. Crediting them for their current success.

Giving credit where credit is due is rare in the business world. But that's good news for marketers because it's an untapped resource for creating a community that markets for you.

FACT: "On average, 76% of shoppers felt closer and more positive about a company after seeing their custom content." –*OnBoardly.com*

5. Twist the traditional.

There's nothing more captivating than experiencing something nostalgic with a new twist. The Piano Guys have done a magnificent job of making us say, "I love that song, and I swear they just made it better." Many of us can whistle the song "So Happy Together" and think of a fond time in life associated with that classic tune. But true to their style, The Piano Guys took that wistfulness to a whole new level by using that recognizable melody to bring their cello to life! Thus, creating a revitalized life moment to refresh our "once was" memory, making it new with an affinity for their brand.

GENIUS!

FACT: It's time to take video seriously! "Americans are watching increasing numbers of videos online. According to *ComScore*, this number has jumped over 43% to 100 million daily views (that's roughly one-third of the U.S. population watching a video online each day)." @ SMexaminer

6. Don't be afraid to say "No!"

The Piano Guys said "no" in a serious way. Believe it or not, this talented group of dads turned down Sony Music **seven times** before signing a contract for a national tour!

It's no secret that these gentlemen are, first and foremost, devoted to their families. "They wanted to make it, but not at the expense of their personal lives" was the quote (expressed in the article, "The Piano Guys are Playing all the Right Keys!") that summed up why they repeatedly turned down Sony. Yes, they have dreams to create even more and said, "We have to do it piecemeal and take it one bite at a time, but eventually, we'd really like to showcase the most incredible places on the earth."

In their 2021 debut celebrating every video they've ever made, viewers can virtually travel the globe in the 16-minute compilation featuring the incredible places they've made magical music. As one of their 7-million subscribers, we're a passionate community who can't wait to see where they go next.

But even with all their hard-earned success, they carefully balance their goals with the next best steps forward. The greatest takeaway is that their ability to balance their priorities has allowed them to "have it all!" Of course, their "all" is just a bit different than traditional expectations, but their fans admire them for it, which creates an even stronger affinity to their family branding concept.

FACT: "What's highest and best for you is always what's highest and best for everyone around you." @MarieForleo

7. Be strategic about partnerships.

From Plácido Domingo to David Archuleta, The Piano Guys partnered with popular performers who not only brought their creative compilations to life but significantly expanded their audience. That's "influencer marketing," a form of marketing that emerged from a variety of recent practices and studies, in which messaging focus is placed on specific key individuals to build influence among an untapped market.

The Piano Guys played the piano upside down on a floating island surrounded by fire and on the Great Wall of China. They've played the cello on a bike, dangling above Mozart in a metal cage while swinging through the air, and on vast salt flats. But it was well-timed, well-planned influencer partnerships that strategically catapulted their popularity in between such jaw-dropping feats. Their robust sense of adventure aligned with their handpicked team and played an assist in developing the influencer's reputation as well.

FACT: Influencers are people with significant networks (followers, readers, etc.) who can speak to a broad range of products and services with the ability to sway opinions in their favor.

NOTES

Chapter 6

YOU CAN MARKET ANYTHING

Remember when I said I was surprised that my favorite class at the University of Florida turned out to be Mass Communication Theory? That's because it's where I learned you can market absolutely anything. Yes, even bad products like the #4 worst product of all time — Clarion Touch of Yogurt Shampoo.

Could you market that?

In its heyday, the product made $8 billion the year it was released to the public in 1979. So yeah, it's possible to market anything if you know who you're talking to.

Now that we've fleshed out the difference between marketing and sales, it's crucial to further drive home that marketing doesn't always mean selling. In its truest form, marketing is the management of profitable relationships, and in relationship management, you aren't always selling; you're building trust!

There's absolutely nothing worse than scrolling through the feed of my favorite platform when I'm suddenly interrupted by some random advertisement. But that's the #1 priority of social platforms with a model geared toward advertisers.

At this point, most business owners would stop me in my tracks and say, "Without advertising, how would we sell anything?"

Through building trustworthy relationships over time, that's how! It takes time! A lot of time, and that's *not* what businesses want to hear. But if you're going to be around in ten years, why not start building in the consistency now to guarantee you'll still be here later?

The hard truth to face is this: **Social isn't for selling, it's for building trust.**

Using social for selling before we use it to build consumer trust is the single most selfish thing organizations can do to harm their most valuable asset—consumer loyalty.

This is where we get into the weeds regarding the disconnect between marketing and sales. Marketers don't always understand that the sales team is operating within a finite amount of time. While marketers spend lots of time perfecting every message, digital cue, and tracking mechanism—sales don't normally have the time to sell what marketers create. So, they wing it and often keep marketing out of the process.

Wrong! The two need to function in unison, leveraging their strengths to optimize the end result. Sales and marketing must explicitly understand each other's roles. To accomplish that usually results in being situated in close proximity, providing cross-training, and meeting consistently. Neither are in control of the customer but possess tools to help influence the decision-making process.

It's tough to know when to pump the brakes on getting your "product" in front of the billions of people who use Facebook, Instagram, LinkedIn, Twitter, or TikTok as their primary sources of communication. But team alignment is crucial to long-term success. Being on social media is not a magic pill a business can swallow to have "all eyes" on them. It's a tool (a pretty powerful one at that) to help build your business in a relevant way for the century we live in. And both teams need to understand how their role contributes to each other.

You start by learning how to use social media to communicate, and you'll actually learn how to use these potent tools to your advantage. But don't use it solely to vocalize a sales message to the masses or skew a narrative in your favor. While most businesses are at the mercy of social media, you don't have to be.

I've managed social platforms for 10 companies in 10 different industries over the past 10 years. Never once has a single person flocked to any of those businesses the moment I made their presence known on social media. But growth was achieved by consistently weaving story-based relationship prompts into the overall marketing strategy—both online and off. That's not because social platforms are magic; it's because I listened to each of their core audiences, made adjustments to their needs, and served up content in a methodical manner that made customers feel heard and part of the process.

Here's how I made that happen:

1. **Follow the 70/20/10 posting ratio rule**. Knowing what to post on each and every social platform can be tricky. Follow this simple rule to create a social environment filled with meaningful engagement that leads to customer action. We will dive into how to do this, in a later chapter.

2. **Prove you care**. Don't ignore the customer service evolution happening within the confines of social media. Sorry, but that does include *publicly addressing negative feedback*. Solving problems in the open is the best way

to show your company is genuinely concerned and the quickest way to win customers for life. Please don't delete a comment because it makes you feel uncomfortable.

3. **Be Social!** Social media is so much more than a trending communications fad. It's an effective platform to get to know your customers and how your product/service can enrich their lives. **Talk with them, not at them.** The sentiment behind this topic is discussed all throughout this book.

4. **Ask customers for ideas**. It's no surprise that social media marketing has exposed weaknesses in a company's ability to connect with customers in a meaningful way. According to Shoutlet's latest findings, "Our research reveals that the best way for brands to get their messages heard by millennials is to market **with** them, not **at** them." But, how the heck do you market with them? You'll learn how to do that as well.

5. **Host Contests**. This is a quick and easy way to build up the target audience you're seeking to isolate. Implement your content infrastructure and a clear goal well before your legal giveaway. Yes, social platforms have specific guidelines to follow when conducting contests, so know the rules! The easiest way to stay clear of violating platform guidelines is to host the contest/giveaway on your website and use social media to drive traffic to your site.

6. **Integrate offline connectivity**. Host events, give back to the community, visit local businesses, engage in radio talk shows, podcasts, and YouTube channels. Establish reasons to build better relationships, not just push a message in front of the face of an unknown customer. Find your customers and get to know them!

Consumer behavior is evolving, and I'm not the only one who's experienced how the relationship-based social phenomenon is causing marketers to take notice.

A few of my fellow marketing friends feel the same way and even have their own insightful twists to add.

Kimba Cooper, Owner at **Kimba Digital Marketing:**
"People use social media and other online platforms to feel like they are part of a community and to build relationships with others. The best marketers have always utilized the skill of building relationships to attract clients or sell products. It's one of the things I love most about Social. You truly see people and businesses for what they are, and some companies are really benefiting as a result."

While **Helen Blunden** of **Activate Learning** unearthed something a tad alarming:
"When interviewing business owners last year, I discovered they had no interest in their staff to use any social media networks for relationship building. Their comments were "they'll not use it for work purposes mainly" or "not on my time and money." However, they did all want social media marketing to be used. But, push marketing—not engagement centric marketing.

Brandon Cox, Director of Marketing at **LynnGroup:**
"In a sense, yes. We're more personal with audiences than ever before. As a result, we have a responsibility to understand the person we're marketing to—especially where they are in the journey. With more data than ever before, it's no longer good enough to blast a generic message across the entire funnel (it really never should have been "good enough"). We have to take a DemandGen view and focus less on LeadGen. This requires knowing who you're marketing to and understanding them through relationship—be it social media, email, content viewing habits, what have you."

Landra Lynn Jacobs, Owner – Digital Marketing Consultant:
"While an increased ability to reach more people quickly is great, that means there's more noise than ever before. To cut through and really get your target market's attention, you have to provide value from the very beginning. This is where marketing has truly changed. Once you realize giving value without strings leads to sales, then you can succeed in today's marketplace."

Mitzi Eaker, Owner – Digital Marketing Consultant:
"Over the next ten years, we will continue to see a decline of the bigger so-

cial media platforms—Facebook, Twitter, LinkedIn, etc. As individuals seek to protect their privacy, personal information, and mental health, we will see an exodus from the big platforms to trusted small niche platforms that connect people with like-minded individuals and brands. I see similar to the old "blog rolls." Marketers will need to help brands define themselves and evolve over time through their content marketing while developing strategic partnerships in order to authentically connect within their market."

So how do you market anything in an ever-changing landscape?

Marketing, simply put, is showing people the value of what you're offering. Whether you're selling an electronic gadget, a business idea, or the benefits of yogurt-infused shampoo, you need to communicate the value of your product in a way that makes your target customer say, "That relates to me, I need that!"

How do you do that?

It's a lot simpler than you think. You have to know what you're marketing, to whom you're marketing, and how to create a lasting connection with your customers. As echoed throughout this book, the formula is relatively simple:

Know the product, understand your customer, set up tracking measurements, and market for the future.

Living and breathing each of these allows you to anticipate customer needs, react, and stay ahead of any competition.

Is New Marketing Really Better Marketing?

One topic I've already touched on and plan to attack from all sides is whether new marketing ideas really make for better marketing.

I've probably asked myself that question a hundred times over the years.

As marketers and business leaders, have you?

If you have, what's your conclusion?

Although I can't yet boast some incredible breakthrough on the matter, I can say that I'm headed in that direction. And you know how relentless I am about getting to the bottom of something! It's only a matter of time. If you haven't already started to reframe your thoughts on what's happening in the marketing industry today, it's time for that too!

For most marketers, we're currently overwhelmed, overworked, and under-delivering as we struggle to keep up with the never-ending stream of new marketing tools. It's a hard thing to admit internally, never mind say out loud. But the consumer data staring us in the face is undeniable. So wouldn't quick solutions provide better options?

According to a 2013 *Inc.* article titled "4 Things Your Customers **Don't** Want," we learn that near the top of that list is—**being sold to**, which was nearly a decade ago! Now, close to ten years later, we're still trying to shove an antiquated sales approach down our customers' throats as quickly and conveniently (for us marketers) as possible. Consumers are WAY beyond tired of being sold to. They want access to real solutions to real problems, and they want to be part of the process.

So, what are we doing about it?

It's our job as marketers to figure this out! Businesses depend on us; heck, consumers depend on us. Marketers can look at the current state of industry operations, consider it, and adjust or continue to underperform. We must do the work to regain our footing. You've picked up this book, so chances are you're looking for answers as well.

With hundreds of social platforms boasting billions of users, there's a never-ending demand for increased digital savvy. Unfortunately, our attempts to achieve that monopolize our time and cloud our judgment.

One of the biggest challenges marketers face is time. We all need to squeeze just a few extra hours out of our day to accomplish a mounting to-do list while performing a 24/7 job. Not to mention finding the time to master marketing communications through the nuances of some of the world's most-used amplification tools.

In many cases, we fall short because let's be real, we don't think we have the time to learn each rising platform's language and use each uniquely. It's one of the main reasons we struggle to gain brand visibility and feel overwhelmed by the content creation process. But it doesn't have to be that way. Marketers don't have to feel defeated by the vast social platforms available.

A thriving multichannel marketing strategy that doesn't feel like you're always a step behind begins and ends with understanding your customers better. As you've learned, it's not just about their demographics (age, gender, income, geographical location) but their psychographics (lifestyle, aspirations, mindset) as well. If we focused more on customers and less on tackling new trends, I'm convinced that we wouldn't feel the overwhelming burden of having to always "keep up."

We must trust that our customers will lead us in the right direction, help us make better decisions, and ultimately become an extension of our marketing efforts.

But in reality, we have very few examples of effective multichannel crowdsourcing marketing efforts. The ones I've seen are largely ignored by consumers. Mark

Schaefer talks in-depth about the phenomenon in his book, *Marketing Rebellion*. Here, he explains the shifting consumer trends that marketers can no longer avoid.

"Marketing is going through an existential crisis. The biggest challenge, we are falling so far behind on everything, and things aren't working the way they used to. The world is moving way ahead. But marketers are not!"

So, it's not about applying a tech-savvy marketing approach to mend our fractured industry. It's about authentically forming a deeper customer connection across multiple touchpoints to create balance and collaboration across the marketing industry.

Know the product, understand your customer, and communicate into the future.

Rinse.

Repeat.

This foundation applies to every marketing scenario on every platform and in every customer communication. All marketers should be able to articulate this in their sleep.

In terms of the future, consider this. With over 2 billion users, Facebook is not guaranteed to be here in another ten years.

Remember Myspace?

Depending on how old you are, you may not either. Once a popular, well-trafficked, international social platform, today, its relevance is reduced to not much more than the role it played as society's first significant attempt at public digital communication.

How about Meerkat, Google+, Vine, or iTunes Ping?

Now all low traffic and, in some cases, long forgotten.

That doesn't mean I have insider tips on the future of Facebook or any other platform. I'm just realistic about the statistical likelihood that a platform will come and go based on its capacity to understand what customers want. A platform's longevity is never a guarantee. That's why your social media use strategy should focus on what's holding your customer's attention.

As marketers, we must keep our eyes open and our motives in check. It's about our ability to leverage the current tools to build a stronger connection that leads to a robust and enduring customer relationship. And that means customers will be platform agnostic. They'll continue to engage with us regardless of the initial platform we engaged on or what platforms pop up in the future. We can achieve this as long as we can figure out how to stop talking *at* them.

As marketers, our plan cannot default to "because everyone else is using it right now." I mean, is your customer even using that platform you're trying to convince your boss to be on? Then, when you do jump on said platform, what's your plan to connect and leverage the relationship into something more mutually beneficial? Something long-lasting? What strategy are you building around your presence there?

Let's say your customer is a female photographer between the age of 20 and 25 who spends her mornings at yoga, afternoons with clients or editing, and evenings networking at art exhibits with her friends. In that case, you most likely won't find her active on LinkedIn but on Instagram instead.

However, if your customer is a 45 to 55-year-old mid-manager male looking to staff his growing ad agency, you have an excellent chance of entering into a conversation with him on LinkedIn.

Know your customer and adapt your strategy around them. Don't get caught in the lie that it's the other way around.

Thankfully, we are knee-deep in the age of technology and have access to data-driven tools that allow us to pose the right questions to the right people to formulate specific customer trends into realistic marketing solutions. The beauty of having such a deep understanding of your audience is you can be where your audience is. It takes all the headache, guesswork, and confusion out of having to master the plethora of available social tools and allows marketers to spend precious time where it matters: communicating with actual customers and those who influence your customer base.

Okay, great! Let's say you fully understand your audience and can articulate the full details of their demographics and psychographics.

What's next?

NOTES

Chapter 7

STELLAR CONTENT = ORGANIC ENGAGEMENT

Now, it's time to take advantage of the communication options across your audience's preferred platforms.

Where do you start?

The easiest and most cost-effective way to make that happen is through stellar content creation! And the way to determine whether you truly have stellar content is to monitor your organic engagement rate. If your organic engagement reaches levels of 60%, you know you've more than hit the mark.

First, you have to know what your current organic reach is and then monitor month over month. Increased organic engagement means your fan base is increasing, and their interactions (likes, comments, shares) are increasing in turn. This increase is a healthy indicator that your content is resonating with your audience.

The tricky part is accomplishing that without posting the same content across every media outlet. Using multiple platforms to further a marketing strategy is about developing a seamless user experience in their preferred digital environment, not a duplicate experience on each and every one.

Our ability to identify the why behind the customer purchase process—not just the how—determines marketing success.

However, content can't just be created for content's sake. Each piece must be considered interconnected touchpoints that represent what customers can expect from doing business with you. For that reason, the content created must be carefully analyzed and executed to deliver maximum engagement results.

There are many different ways to create, use, and distribute content to convey the right messages. The question then is, do we currently have examples of successful multichannel marketing campaigns to learn from?

Of course, we do! The best examples I've seen so far are simple conversations that draw a niche target market further into a private (yet valuable) discussion on a particular topic that interests them. Gary Vaynerchuck calls it—The Content

Model—and in a 2019 article, he shared the mindset behind crafting such a content strategy. He said:

"Mastering content strategy, creation, and distribution for your brand on social media is a difficult and long process. But the following reverse pyramid model starts with a piece of pillar content. This could take many different forms — for example, if you're not comfortable on video, you could record a podcast. You might even film yourself recording the podcast so you could have a video out of it as well. Then, from that pillar video or audio clip, you can create content for your website and subsequent media platforms."

It's called micro-content: small bits and blurbs are taken from the larger pillar piece to tell an interconnected story in bite sizes. The following is from a PowerPoint that Gary and his team put together to help empower and potentially completely shift how you think about producing and distributing content online for your brand.

Watch the @GaryVee Content Model – "How I make 30+ pieces of content from a single keynote" for more guidance.

The Content Pyramid

Start with one long-form piece of content, one long video or show in which all other content is derived.

Next, re-purpose into micro-content. Create short-form content like articles, memes, images, quotes, stories, mashups, remixes, rants, gifs, etc.

Finally, distribute across the media channels where your target audience is most active, adapting to the platform each content piece fits within organically.

The first round of micro-content is ultimately used to drive viewership to the original pillar content, which, in turn, should be set up to convert visitors to take action with you.

Now, the most critical piece of all—*it's time to listen!* After you've distributed your pillar and micro-content, listen to your audience to determine what content most resonated with them. Monitor and respond to comments. Find trends among those who share. Once you've decided which were the best-performing content pieces, plan to develop more of that content. Then repeat the process. This refinement process is key to learning how to provide value to your audience.

THE CONTENT PYRAMID

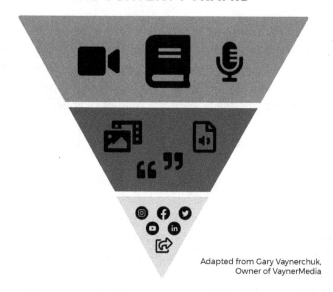

Adapted from Gary Vaynerchuk,
Owner of VaynerMedia

When Gary first used this model, he turned one keynote into 30 pieces of content, sharing a variety of content across many major online platforms, resulting in 35 million views. You can find the pillar piece of content he used for this study online by typing in "Optimism or Pessimism? You choose. | on YouTube- Dailyvee #316."

So why isn't every marketer using results-based content tactics?

Marketers from the tippy-top to the very bottom of the totem pole face the same hurdle: **turning a multichannel strategy into human connections**. It's not about how well you know technology or your ability to wield the tools; it's all about our willingness to learn more, understand, and listen to the target audience. When that's the true focus, the appropriate multichannel options naturally emerge based on what's best for that particular audience.

So, how can brands leverage the vast social media platforms to further their marketing agenda? Easy! Marketers need to find more ways to use marketing tools to foster human touchpoints and not focus so much on automation to increase sales. Forget the bandwagon and work on genuinely connecting and communicating with customers, and you'll ALWAYS win at marketing regardless of what digital tools come and go.

The truth is, we can't really say if new marketing is better marketing until we have mastered foundational marketing tactics first, and that's what this whole book is about.

Technical Examples.

I'm usually knee-deep in, well, something other than watching TV. But that's one of the ways my husband likes to stay connected amid our chaotic life, cuddled up and experiencing a story together. A story in motion picture format, of course. So, when my husband first asked me to watch the movie *Chef*, I was soon delighted to find I could spend time with two of my great loves: my husband and marketing. My mind constantly operates through a marketing lens, so I soon became aware that the progressive tactics portrayed in this film were so imaginatively innovative that I couldn't pass up the opportunity to dissect the amazing marketing strategies that soon emerged.

Beyond the sheer marketing genius, there are many lessons to be learned. The movie is packed with so many ideas; I could have easily written three other chapters just from the creative spark it ignited. And if I did, I'd name them something like, "If a 10-Year-Old Ran Your Social Strategy," or "Twitter: At Least a 10-Year-Old Can Do It" or "How to Recover from a Negative Tweet Gone Viral." Who knows, those just may end up as a future book.

But for now, we'll dive right into "**The 20 Steps That Built a Massively Responsive online Community Around a Simple Product.**"

1. **Start with a unique, yet simple product**. Don't make the mistake of thinking your product or service is here to please the masses. Instead, perfect what makes you unique, even if it's just one thing, and be consistent with it.

2. **Keep your profile pictures refreshed**. If the mood changes, show it—literally—with a profile update. One of the reasons people are addicted to social media is because of all the constant real-time updates. It's no wonder sterile websites lose substantial traffic to social platforms due to their "freshness factor."

3. **Tell the behind-the-scenes story**. Being transparent is quickly becoming one of the best ways to expedite the growth of your online community and develop deeply rooted brand loyalty. Companies that involve their communities in the good, bad, and ugly of the day-to-day grind are seeing pretty impressive results and producing a passionate following as a result.

4. **Give away free products**. It's all about give and take; find a way to do it creatively by representing your human side by offering more than anyone else in your industry.

5. **Be confident in decision-making**. Realize that not every decision will be the right one. In fact, you'll feel crippled operating your business as if you're walking on eggshells. Be confident and stand behind your status updates and defend them boldly!

6. **Test your new ideas**. In the movie, the food truck owners tested their simple menu on a diverse crowd. Stop making business decisions entirely on your own. Marketing allows you to crowdsource decisions through your community reach. Wondering if something will work? Before spending money on it, ask your community what they think, then monitor and interact with their feedback.

7. **Have a comeback story**. Have you blown it online? Great! Use it as a way to rekindle your passion, improve your product, and create redemption. People love it! I mean, people fail, but it doesn't have to mean it's time to close up shop and start again.

8. **Create fun, brand-relevant graphics**. We are way past text-only updates. Since 90% of information transmitted to the brain is visual, take advantage of the many free tools to jazz up your photos to create visual content.

9. **Make an in-the-moment photo or video**. Take advantage of the fact that the "us-sie" is the new autograph! Encourage followers to snap those shutters during those fun "behind the scenes" moments. Have you met Instagram? This is how customers are expecting to interact with your business, but businesses just aren't showing up.

10. **Exhibit a grateful attitude toward customers**. When is the last time you said, "thank you?" It doesn't cost anything, and it perpetuates value like nothing else. Finding ways to show that you would be nothing without your fans is more valuable than a sale and inspires millennials to talk about your brand online.

11. **Interact with your community**. If people love what you do, revel in it and find a way to authentically become a part of their day. Making meaningful connections that build a vocal community really matters!

12. **Refer Twitter users to your videos**. If you're more active on TikTok or Instagram, find ways to move your Twitter users over to follow you there as well. That reveals another side of your business and strengthens the relationships you're building. Remember not to join these communities with a sales-focused agenda. *Read Jab, Jab, Jab Right Hook* and learn how to use any platform genuinely.

13. **Turn on locations**. (geotag) Geo-location marketing is changing the not-so-distant marketing future. Get in the habit of geo-locating your status updates so nearby folks can find you while they're in your vicinity. They aren't looking at that street sign ad; they're scrolling their phone to see if there's a local experience they can be a part of. Be that experience!

14. **Give credit where credit is due**. Has a customer written a blog post about you? Shared your info with their Facebook group? Wrote a YouTube review? Please recognize them and do something that will blow them away. Find out what their favorite restaurant is and send them a gift card. That's money better spent than on an ad to the masses. Find a way to make your followers feel special, one at a time. The social tool, Mention, can help you find the online conversations or "mentions" you don't even know you're ignoring.

15. **Plan ahead**. For anyone to take you seriously online, you must be consistent. Being consistent requires having a plan. Find time every week to plan your posts for the upcoming week. Be ready with what you want to say and leave room to also say it in real-time.

16. **Situate yourself as a community staple**. Become part of the ambiance of a community as an integral entity without interrupting your customer's life.

17. **Understand the community impact**. You must know how your business ecosystem affects your community by understanding the psychographics of your target market.

18. **Have fun and be yourself**. That's all...seriously. You are unique, and that's why you will succeed. Not because you're copying what the "experts" are doing.

19. **Make an unexpected partnership**. Partnerships are another marketing trend that interests me. In the podcast *Marketing Partnerships: How to Extend Your Reach with Content Collaboration*, Andrew Davis explains in great detail how strategic partnerships are more powerful than traditional marketing tactics. Just like we saw with The Piano Guys.

20. **Do what makes you happy without the pressure to sell/succeed**. Run your business as if you were not dependent upon the money you make. It takes the pressure off of being overly sales-focused and builds the trust and authenticity customers are desperate for!

In any strategy changes you adapt, make sure they first accompany your overall marketing plans. But at the same time, don't be scared to experiment to see what does and does not work.

Then, apply these content garnering concepts against the 70/20/10 posting rule and you'll be in the business of better marketing that talks directly to customers!

And now that you've basically watched the movie through my marketing lens, watch it for real and share your perspective with me anywhere on social media! FYI, this film is rated R and not recommended for a young audience.

NOTES

Chapter 8

UNDERSTANDING AND UPHOLDING ETHICS

When it comes to poor marketing practices, you certainly don't want to be part of the problem. So, understanding whether you are or not is paramount to becoming "Made to Market." I could barrage you with examples of poor practices flooding the market space, but what if we focused on making a positive impact instead?

When you join fellow marketers already engaged in high standards, you create a unified front that is much more difficult to break down. So it's our responsibility to educate ourselves on what is right and wrong, then take reasonable action according to a set of guidelines based on the best interest of our fellow humans.

Like in any industry, marketing professionals are responsible for maintaining a high standard of service and support within the field. We'll discuss ethical marketing practices and where to draw the line while still leaving plenty of room for creative and compelling messaging.

First, answer the following question in the notes section of this chapter:

As a marketer, do I operate ethically? Why/Why not?

Whether you work in a marketing department or for yourself, a solid bold line should be drawn around how you compel a customer to take action. Instead of nit-picking about what's right and wrong in marketing, let's look at two-sided examples to better illustrate ethics in marketing. If you work by yourself, on a group team, or play a leadership role, you need to know how to make ethical decisions based on *actual* ethical standards **and** *perceived* ethical standards expressed by consumers.

When does marketing cross an ethical line?

Out of the options surveyed in a *Marketing Charts* report, it's clear that the 400 marketers who participated in this survey feel that ethical marketing means telling the truth and providing transparency to customers. Okay, we seem to be on the same page. But if that's what's really happening, why did 69% of consumers cite the top ongoing unethical practice of **marketing that distorts or exaggerates the truth?**

What's an exaggeration or distortion of your company's truth?

Overall, this report shows exaggeration, lack of transparency, exploiting vulnerable groups, canceling information, and shaming into action are among the top offenders of unethical marketing. While an overwhelming majority (92%) of marketers consider themselves ethical, according to research released by *Phrasee*, the same study also reveals that one-fourth have been pressured to use unethical marketing tactics at work.

Pressured? By who? The boss? Team members?

Marketers should be armed with enough knowledge of the psychological effects of marketing and social pervasiveness to understand where to draw the line. Those being easily "pressured" either know better and are only looking out for their jobs or aren't informed enough to know where, how, and when to push back and hold the ethical line. As a marketer, you can easily justify to leadership why you engage in canceling or avoidance behavior. But when a customer has a negative experience as a result of canceling or avoiding a topic in your favor, try to use that same justification on them. It'll be met with contention every time!

Check out how unethical marketing looks and feels from a consumer perspective.

"Airlines that advertise low fares when the actual cost is double or more, as they charge extras for breathing, getting on the plane, bringing luggage, water, early boarding, etc."

"Hotels that charge $30 to $50 a night for the use or non-use of their tiny treadmills, lousy Wi-Fi, and a pond out back to swim in."

"All utilities, which have so many surcharges that a lawyer doesn't even understand."

"Any government agency that takes two hours to answer a phone, along with a wonderful trip to the SSA to speak to their overburdened agents, who lecture you for not providing a blood sample, and your firstborn, to get any kind of document you might need."

"Exaggerating or distorting the truth is anything but truthful. It's a lie. Lie to me, and I'll never do business with you again. I once worked with a printer who told me my project would be done by a certain date. He missed it by a significant number of days. When pressed, he openly admitted that he knew if he told me the truth—as in how long the job would take—that I would go to a competitor. He was right. The next time I needed something printed, that's exactly where I went. Any distortion of the truth is a lie. Marketers that hype beyond the truth are unethical."

"Fashion ads whittle off inches and enhance body parts. Beauty ads erase pores and wrinkles, even tear ducts. How anyone can believe beauty product claims these days is beyond me. It is time to lose the filters and put real people in ads.

I don't know about you, but I want to see what a product can really do, not the Photoshopped version of what it's selling it wants to do."

"I always hated negative opt-in — if you don't tell us you don't want the book of the month, you get the book of the month. Same today with "free trials" in digital. You enter your credit card, and the subscription will start past the trial period unless you cancel, but it becomes really hard sometimes to figure out how to cancel (often no customer service number is even available). I guess this falls into the theme of giving consumers the illusion of control."

These just scratch the surface of a scathing consumer opinion poll. Think about it, though. All of their examples have become a part of everyday life for most of us!

So, if normal touchpoints from major organizations result in negative customer perceptions about their marketing ethics, how is it possible that 92% of marketers truly operate ethically? Talk about a major disconnect!

And this dismal view stretches to how consumers view industry professionals. Gallup surveys consistently show that advertising practitioners are among the least trusted professionals for honesty and ethics—ranked among car salespeople and members of Congress. We all know there are good ones out there and I certainly feel their pain on having to fight a bias battle, but we're talking consumer perception, which is their reality.

Are you appalled yet? I am!

Nobody wants to be perceived that way, so it's our responsibility to fight for our customers! Let's start with transparency. Customers should be privy to all aspects of a product, not just the ones that increase company profit. As marketers, we're responsible for maintaining those standards and incorporating them in content while addressing customer needs. We work hard to uncover genuine problems that should be addressed by genuine solutions. Don't waste time and compromise your integrity by trying to spin it some other way.

Spinning a Story

Although we've learned that we can, in fact, market anything, that doesn't mean it's okay to spin the story however we see best to sell said product. We can't neglect essential details that may be the deciding factor in a purchasing decision.

In my last position, I was the Jackson County Tourism Director in Northeastern Alabama, where the lower Appalachian foothills begin, on Alabama's largest lake. This mountain lake region borders Georgia and Tennessee at its tippy-top northeast corner of the state and is stunningly beautiful, even on its worst day.

The landscape beckons me to proclaim this is an outdoor mecca that I wish was ripe with an abundance of well-worn hiking trails, creative camping options, the cutest and most eclectic mom-and-pop restaurants, flanked by a luscious lakeside winery experience. But we're not quite there yet.

So, when it comes to accessing the thousands of public acres, our area's current story is about the wild outdoors and expansive cave system that visitors can explore on their own. I would tell them where to go, how to be prepared, and then send them on their way. Our area caters to the outdoor adventure enthusiast who is okay trekking out in the wilderness on their own. Sure, there are a handful of places to rent kayaks, but there are no mountain bike trails or niche breweries to boast about yet, and visitors have told us repeatedly that we lack dining options.

Knowing all that, I remained cautious about how I promote the area because the last thing I wanted is for a visitor to come with a heightened expectation that we can't live up to. A disappointed visitor will not be a return visitor. With a goal to build a better visitor experience, here's how I accurately presented our tucked-away mountain lake region.

"Here, you can explore the wilder side of the tri-state area. Find your own adventure in clean peace and discover seclusion that's rare in neighboring urban areas."

I use high-quality video and photos to show exactly what the area looks like and leave it to the traveler to create their own itinerary. I prompt with suggestions located throughout our region, highlight our lodging options and show the behind-the-scenes of what outdoor adventuring really looks like over on the @TrailTherapyAL Instagram page.

We have hard-to-access waterfalls, highly regulated and heavily permitted caves, and protected public land. But I am honest about it all and create new ways to easily access the outdoors by building relationships with area businesses and local leaders. Engaging in much more marketing than that at this time would not be accurate. So a lot of time is focused on building a social presence that keeps locals and visitors talking up what we have now or include them in the development of what they'd like to one day experience.

I've learned how to speak to the outdoor adventurers who want that kind of getaway, and I will not disappoint them. While here, they'll find something they can't experience in many other places in the Southeast. While here, the experience they have will determine not only if they come back, but maybe if they decide to one day become a resident—investing in the community. Longer-term communication results in action. That's marketing!

If I build a promotional expectation that disappoints, I can forget about converting lifelong touchpoints.

This way, as we grow, our outdoor adventure offerings will grow, and so will the number of times visitors choose to return.

But my actions aren't by accident. They follow objective standards of message crafting to convert loyal customers. *According to the AMA Code of Conduct, the number one standard for marketing practitioners is "Do no harm."* This means consciously avoiding harmful actions, including omissions, by embodying high ethical standards and adhering to all applicable laws and regulations in the choices we make. The omission of pertinent information is just as harmful as openly misleading customers; those you're trying to convert are painfully aware of what's going on.

"Should I?" vs. "Could I?"

My question is, how many marketers ask, "should I?" instead of "could I?"

When marketing becomes a job thrust upon you as the youngest person in the office, I don't believe the "should" question gets asked, let alone answered. In this scenario, marketing becomes a unicorn that only the young and tech-savvy can conjure to drive more sales. By now, you know that's not true, but when "only the young and tech-savvy..." becomes the focus and method for execution, questionable ethics are guaranteed. A tricky question to answer, especially when someone else pays you to focus on sales growth. But, as marketers, we have a responsibility.

When is it too much?

Movies like the Netflix-based documentary, *The Social Dilemma*, and books like *The Age of Surveillance Capitalism* unveil the sobering fact that "the technology that connects us also controls, manipulates, monetizes, divides, and distracts us." In it, we learn, *"Never before have a handful of tech designers had such control over the way billions of us think, act, and live our lives."* The mental health, democracy, and discrimination dilemmas set forth by the creators of this film have marketers wondering how much data, how much tracking, how much listening is too much?

We need to understand the difference between technology and surveillance capitalism and their role in ethical marketing—two very different things, with two very different outcomes that are intricately woven into a marketer's day-to-day operations. As marketers, we need to be hyper-focused on our use of technology in ethical ways, not in ways that gobble up data to mislead and manipulate the public.

The purpose and methods of data collection matter in a marketing strategy, making the setup of privacy parameters paramount to building trust. We want to inform and assure our customers when they consent to how their data is used.

Clear identification and legal guidelines must indicate that data collection is solely to improve products or services that directly impact the customer whose data you're collecting.

For example, Apple has drawn a clear line around data collection for an all-inclusive customer experience rather than surveillance capitalism and is engaged in a mighty battle with Facebook as a result. Only time will tell how this will affect us all.

Consumer Psychology

Something you'll often hear me say is, marketing is 50% analytical and 50% psychology. We're dealing with the potential to manipulate human emotions for a specific outcome—while trying to build trust and revenue. My personal stance: I don't want to manipulate at all. Ever. Especially not when I'm the last line of defense between a personal financial decision and company profit. If I stand clear of the ethical line, I don't have to worry about stepping over it, even by accident.

That's why learning the psychology of your customer is so important. The idea of someone hounding me until I finally "give in" just to get them off my back is something I refuse to be associated with. Employers expecting similar outcomes should raise red flags for marketers, and vice versa.

Right about now, you may be thinking, "Oh dang! I'm guilty of that, now what?"

I learned this tactic in the military. If you've ever experienced bootcamp, you know what I'm talking about. Drill sergeants are trained to completely break you mentally and emotionally to make soldiers malleable enough to be compliant teammates in all situations encountered in military life. It's this harsh balance of correction and confidence-building that keeps soldiers assured, working well together, and safe in a wartime situation. In marketing, we need to be just as unified, maintaining the front lines of an industry built to significantly impact every business sector on planet earth. So, let's retrain our brain and our actions to function ethically while still operating in a creative-rich realm of messaging and trust-building.

Don't beat yourself up over operating obliviously, but let's build you back up with examples of current creative, ethical marketing. The following represent eight lessons I learned from Chris Erthel on ethical advertising messaging that you can easily apply to your processes. Part of your homework for this chapter includes checking out these examples online and applying their tactics to your marketing knowledge toolbox.

1. Surprise + Humor, like in the thecrunchcup.com commercial

2. Pitch-play-plunge strategy as seen in pretty much every *Shark Tank* pitch

3. User Generated Content, like in the Target "Acceptance" commercial from 2014

4. Founders Passion, like in the Lumē | Can Deodorant Change Your Life commercial

5. Heartbeat Method, like in the The Norvan LD2 Shoe | Arc'teryx Run commercial

6. Pattern Interrupted, like in the Penn & Teller Teach the Art of Magic commercial

7. Bold Statements, like when Spanx CEO Sara Blakely offers advice to redefine failure

8. Questions, like "does your water bottle clean itself? In the LARQ commercial

Now, answer this question again.
As a marketer, do I operate ethically? Why/Why not?

Takeaway: Marketers, we are the gatekeepers between consumers and corporate profit. Consumers rely on us to tell them the truth and provide access to products and services that make their lives better. So what are we doing to ensure that we toe that line?

NOTES

Chapter 9

ANALYTICS, THE SECRET SAUCE

o far, we've talked about issues plaguing the marketing industry, including:

- Inability to communicate with a specific target audience

- Confusing marketing for sales, and vice versa

- Lacking a clear ethical standard in perceived consumer perception

- Seeking out growth hacks and loopholes before learning customer needs

- Lack of a foundationally structured knowledge base to learn from

Structure in marking includes access to analytics, so we must add measuring and analyzing to our list as part of industry solutions. Marketers and businesses lag in this area, consistently. Yet, if you're a marketer seeking employment in an agency or on a corporate marketing team, the role now requires you to have experience with measuring results. Undoubtedly, those hiring authorities understand the importance of measuring marketing efforts. But are marketers truly learning, practicing, and honing this skill? There seems to be a disparity between the demand and availability of this vital modern-day marketing proficiency.

Meet Agorapulse

Like any other trades(wo)man, I rely on specific tools of the trade to support my quest to become a master marketer. To know me is to know I constantly talk about relevant tools of the trade on my blog and social stories. By this point, many friends know the tools I use, and for those who don't, Agorapulse is on the top of my list.

After years of bragging on Agorapulse, Bill, D.C. metro-based sales manager for Bauscher Hepp, Inc., known as @dcplateking on Instagram, reached out and encouraged me to really articulate the "why" behind my reliance on one of my favorite social management tools. I expressed to Bill all the ways I've become a better marketer thanks to this robustly savvy analytics tool, expressing the following points.

You know when you're sitting on something good, great even? It could be an idea, a thought, a bit of info, or even a chair. But it's so wonderful you just have to share? For this chapter, Agorapulse is my chair, and if you're working in the marketing industry and share my passion for better marketing, you'll love this tool!

Although it's been around a while now, the platform is constantly innovating, improving, and adjusting to users. Heck, while writing this, I learned of their new partnership with Canva, which now allows marketers to design posts using Canva directly from their Agorapulse dashboard! As a result, you'll rarely have to leave the platform now!

In addition, these are the top ways Agorapulse has contributed to my success.

1. The ability to measure organic engagement.

Does the following question sound familiar?

"I post stuff on Facebook, but no one ever sees it, so what's the point?"

I hear it all the time! If you're not measuring, if you're measuring the wrong metrics, and/or if you're not taking action on those metrics, you're right, there is no point.

Why measure and tweak in the first place?

Because the correlation between social strategy and increased revenue is the crucial link to determining the success of content creation. Remember how my very first client asked, "What's the return on investment (ROI) for hiring you to manage our online presence?" Well, Agorapulse made it possible to finally answer the all-important question and ensure every client achieved increased ROI benchmarks.

The point is, the rate of fan interaction with your content directly affects your organic engagement rates. In turn organic engagement rates are directly linked to dollars spent with your organization.

The theory really does play out as simply as that.

However, the quality of your content determines whether or not you'll attain that positive correlation. If people aren't engaging, it means you aren't truly speaking to them. Don't worry; I'll address that in-depth when discussing the 70/20/10 rule later in the chapter.

Here's a real-world example why the Agorapulse ROI tool is a foundational anchor for me.

Glass Art Studio Example

When I first started working with a glass art studio in 2017, they averaged an 8% organic engagement rate on Facebook. Not terrible, considering most expert marketers agree that the industry standard is 2.3% on average. Immediately, we made it a goal to hit 15%. Not knowing how long it would take, we created a benchmark, then worked toward it as we adjusted the content creation process based on key performance indicators (KPIs). The studio set the KPIs, which I tracked in monthly engagement reports.

To our delightful surprise, it took us only three months to hit 15% organically, thanks to a highly engaging content plan that spoke directly to their fans. Within six months, organic engagement was 28%. During that same six-month period, we only ran one two-week ad geared toward email sign-ups that drove users off Facebook and onto the studio's website. Other than that, this increase was strictly due to the long-term content process of continuously fine-tuning to bust our goals.

Every month, I saw an ROI dollar amount staring at me in the reports. By the end of the six months, the ROI tool in Agorapulse had calculated an increased $8,000. This suggested they made $8,000 **more** during the six months we worked together than the corresponding six months in the previous year. I'd been looking at that projected ROI for a while, never paying much attention to that report indicator. Then, I asked my client if she could confirm a revenue increase. She said, "Sarah, we actually made $10,000 more!"

In that moment, I realized I'd achieved my most elusive professional goal: to create simple and trackable correlations proving the power of an organization's planned presence on social media.

In black and white, we proved increased profits were due to the content refinement process around increasing organic engagement rates.

Finally! I discovered the "ROI of Social Media" with the assistance of Agorapulse!

2. In-depth reporting capabilities.

Whenever I'm hired, my employer has no clue that I'm armed with secret weapons. With Agorapulse, I can pull monthly reports offering powerful insights into the organization's online presence, data they never knew was possible. This includes the good, bad, and everything in between. Here, I make adjustments based on what the reports reveal. That allows us to follow goals and objectives to completion as we continuously streamline efforts to grow communities that directly impact organizational growth.

I've learned (the hard way) that digital marketing is extremely intangible at times. So, as a marketer finding ways to quantify my work is my mission. Without the assist of Agorapulse, I'm not sure how else I'd prove the worth of my work so accurately. Their reports enable marketers to adjust parameters easily, pull, and present, then concretely verify that social platform-based efforts are time well spent.

Among the many available reports, my favorite is their competitor analyst monitoring capability. For those who wonder:

What your competitors are up to;
Or how your online presence stacks up;
Or how your organic engagement rates compare to industry comparables.

This tool opens up a whole new world of monitoring. Here, you can add up to five competitors to track several important benchmarks, such as engagement rates, likes, interactions, page posts, and fan count.

With my glass art client, we kept an eye on competitors. But honestly, they were already beating all regional competition in social performance, so we used the competitor analysis tool to create long-term goals against those they strived to realize. Kind of like putting a picture of a fitness model on your refrigerator door to remind you of your weight goals; we placed huge industry-related brands in their competitor profile to reach their long-term brand goal.

Every month, when I pulled their report, it reminded us to take a look at what their industry giant partners were doing on social media. We then analyzed their strategy to find creative new ways to push our efforts toward their goal in a way that closed the competitive gap.

3. Flawless team integration.

When I first onboard new clients, I'm often asked, "So, who approves all this content you'll be creating?" Thanks to Agorapulse, my answer is always, "You will!"

Agorapulse assigns "team members" to individual accounts. When you assign members, only they have access to the accounts you want them to access, allowing clients/employers to have the final say on any social content before it goes live in a neatly organized profile.

During the content creation process, I assign every piece of content to my clients for their approval. They see the same calendar format and content that I do. During the initial training process, I teach them that when they see the "yellow dots," that's their prompt that content is waiting for approval. Typically, I send them an email reminder when I'm finished and then offer a deadline for approval. They're able to go in, edit, adjust, reassign, make notes, and approve. This allows me to maintain professional organization in a way that sets me apart from other marketers, allowing us to work virtually with no interruptions or delays.

4. Manage social interactions on one dashboard.

When I say "under one dashboard," I really mean it! Agorapulse's social CRM (customer relationship management) feature gives you control of your social community in deliberate and effective formats. Agorapulse knows who's been most engaged and who's published content about your brand. From the dashboard, you can check, comment, like, and share to all linked accounts. From there, you can even assign influencer status based on viral potential and commitment level, then neatly categorize brand ambassadors with automated badges that are easy to identify and recognize.

Agorapulse is a vital reporting entity of social media marketing, an essential tool that must be part of the overall industry toolbox. Reports enable social media managers to make precise suggestions based on the previous month's results, including engagement rates, best time/day to post, best topics to post about, target market details, and where people are most frequently absorbing content.

Each social account comes with its own inbox to manage, reply, tag posts, comment, private message, reply, and review. Options are available to manage anywhere from 1–20 accounts at any given time.

Monitoring allows you to reply to notifications, assign influencer status, review online mentions of your brand, and flag for content conversation categories — all from within the platform while seamlessly navigating from one account to the next.

Advanced settings allow you to monitor business mentions, specific hashtags, and keyword tracking as well.

Competitor Analysis helps you keep a close eye on the competition in an analytical format. Wondering how your competitors are behaving online? Not anymore.

Under the competitor tab, add up to 5 Facebook pages that are in direct competition with your brand. Every time you request a report, a complete side-by-side comparison is included to fully grasp how your social efforts stack up. This opens up possibilities to solve industry gaps, allowing you to quickly be the one to fill them and stand out from the crowd.

Most Common Marketing Mistakes

With Agorapulse, marketers can now avoid the most common blows wreaking havoc on a business's online presence.

1. Failing to understand your target audience.

The point of any business is to solve a problem. Ask yourself: "Do I know the problem my business solves?" Your answer should be granular and precise. Not, "I help moms who love to cook achieve a work/life balance." But, "Yes, I help female CEO's in Alabama determine how to close their PR Company's client gap using social media within six months." When you don't specifically know the who and why of addressing a customer, each and every social attempt is cast out into the social void. That's when comments like, "I post stuff on Facebook, but no one ever sees it, so what's the point?" are made.

It's no wonder then that only half of all companies fully understand their target market.

Do you?

2. Failing to make a baseline measurement.

If you don't know where you started, how do you know how far you've come? Or if you've moved the needle at all? The social media industry is already shrouded in mistrust because the over-emphasis of vanity metrics doesn't resemble a return on investment. Not even close. But if you apply specific social marketing steps to know where you started and where you went, it's easier to show social's impact on the company's bottom line.

Getting started and need to determine your baseline?

Learn more about it in the article: "Why a Baseline is Essential to Accurate Marketing Attribution," by *Marketing Land*.

3. Too many social networks, not enough content.

Who says you have to be all things to all people? Trying to fill 4-plus social profiles with high-quality content is a colossal task!

You may be surprised that the answer to this is NOT to create and post the same content across all platforms. If you are doing that, please stop immediately!

Instead, research which platforms your customers frequent and find valuable ways to communicate without selling! If your product is what they need, they will buy it. But they aren't on social media to purchase things, so don't make them feel as if that's your sole intention for showing up there via your communication strategy.

4. Ignoring interactions.

This one is easy. Interact with each person that interacts with your brand. Then take it a step further and get to know top interactors with your brand with the Agorapulse influencer badge assignment. Do this every day for a year, and I dare you to tell me that social media does not affect your bottom line.

The results are monumental, and you can find illustrated examples in the book *Thank You Economy* by *New York Times* bestselling entrepreneurial author Gary Vaynerchuk.

5. Moving forward without a plan.

A goal without a plan is just a wish, and building a business that operates effectively online takes more than wishful thinking. Start with a plan and know the proper tools necessary to save your business.

With a report card like this, it's easy to see why Agorapulse just CAN'T be ignored and deserves to take its rightful place as one of the industry's most reputable tools.

By now, it's clear that the professional leaps in my marketing journey wouldn't have been possible without it. In the past, I've tried tools so robust that I didn't know what to do with all the data. You won't have that problem with Agorapulse.

Their promise to "Simplify Social Media Management" is executed with the power to "Harness your social media content and engagement with the easiest and most affordable social media management tool for teams and agencies."

To Emeric and the whole Agorapulse Team: Thank you! Looking forward to discovering what I can accomplish for my clients using your tool for years to come.

Next let's talk about, Google Analytics

Now in its fourth rendition, Google announced its newest version of Analytics at the end of 2020. But what does the new version mean for marketers, and how does it compare to the traditional version? Although I don't consider myself a Google Analytics expert, marketers must keep a pulse on one of the most powerful data tools at our disposal and know which sources to reference as we continue to keep up with industry trends.

One of the biggest differences in Google 4 is the new data modeling feature. It uses artificial intelligence to fill gaps in data where traditional analytics may be blocked by cookie-consent rules, and blocked JavaScript. With a focus on privacy, it's designed to be "future proof" and work in a world without cookies or identifying personal data while traveling the web. It's a big deal, and I'm not going to pretend I know a ton about it. For more in-depth education and how to become a better practitioner of the tool, I suggest following folks like HubSpot, Chris Mercer, Neil Patel, or Rand Fishkin.

Don't worry, we're not about to get tangled up in the weeds of the platform. But, we will look at how marketers should use the tool from a peripheral perspective. Regulatory changes such as the California Consumer Privacy Act (CCPA) and the General Data Protection Regulation (GDPR) have raised the bar for end-user privacy. Businesses are investing in analytics to navigate all the digital transformations in commerce—from privacy to user volume—and according to *Forbes*, 50% of businesses say that big data has fundamentally changed business practices in their marketing department.

Now, let's consider a privacy-centric artificial intelligence (AI) analytics model.

I know that's a mouthful. But its primary goal is to shift the way data focuses on users—resulting in a more private online journey. If you aren't already familiar with Google Analytics, it's time to take notice. You'll want to incorporate this tool in your marketing efforts because everything is changing… again, and it's going to affect your strategic marketing strategy in some way!

From the very beginning, analytics changed the way I marketed, taking my skills to a whole new level. I'm certainly not the only marketer who's experienced this. In a survey from Forrester Consulting, marketers said that improving their use of analytics is a top priority. My advice: don't leave it out of your education or practitioner process.

Anyone working in the field of marketing is clamoring to get an inside scoop behind the mechanics of Google's new advanced machine learning-based platform to gain even the slightest edge over their competition. I'd like to share a behind-the-scenes peek of what I discovered from studying this topic in-depth while completing my master's.

While data is the microlevel of analytics, let's step back and review the macro parts to determine the impact on the data you're collecting. It's important to first gain insight into how Google Search directly affects websites and the data it's collecting.

How does Google Search Work?

So, how does Google Search work? I'll explain it the same way I do when teaching marketing classes, hopefully providing folks with a tangible grasp of how many Google touchpoints we actually have control over.

Let's say (because I don't know for sure) Google has 2,000 bot-centric indicators to determine how to get ranked higher in search engines—marketers only know 100 of those indicators. The other 1,800 are proprietary to the world's data conglomerate, who most likely have few plans to share. So, as marketers, we must know and execute as many of the 100 indicators as possible in order to optimize online brand ranking.

Even the technicalities of how Google functions excite my inner nerd. I imagine how their nifty spiders crawl around in hopes of perfectly matching a company's product/service with the exact topic a user is hoping to find at the speed of light. Did you know that businesses are highly rewarded for being relevant without having to pay? Just look into setting up a "Google my business" to see what I mean.

See, Google's crawling bots are constantly out "organically" searching with the means and mission to match up a relevant product/service with a user. Without the physical submission of your site, it takes a lot more time for the bots to discover and link what you do with the user's needs. A physical site submission lets you skip the indexing line to immediately be placed in the correct categories. That more readily allows the indexing function to produce results on you instead of your competitors.

Although this is a great first step, upon completing your website, that's not all you have to do to rank higher. Based on Google's Webmaster Guidelines, there are quite a few other actions required to make sure Google can crawl and index your site correctly.

Among the 100 known parameters marketers must execute to produce analytics and SEO touchpoints, you'll find the following are at the top of the list.

- Every page should be available through **one** static link

- Indicate page titles by using title tags

- Accurately describe the page's content

- Create unique title tags for each page

- Use brief, but descriptive titles

- Make use of the "description" meta tag

- Accurately summarize the page's content

- Improve the structure of your URLs

- Use words in URLs

- Provide one version of a URL to reach a document

- Make your site easier to navigate

- Plan out your navigation based on your homepage

- Create a naturally flowing hierarchy

- Ensure more convenience for users by using 'breadcrumb lists"

- Make a sitemap available to help users find your most important parts

- Prepare two sitemaps: one for users, one for search engines

- Have a helpful 404 page

- Use heading tags appropriately

- Offer quality content and services

- Write easy-to-read text

- Write better anchor text

- Titles should be descriptive and accurate

- There should be a reasonable number of reference links per page

- Optimize your use of images! Crawlers don't recognize text in images.If you do add text, be sure to add keywords to ALT attributes and descriptions.

Honestly, this is only the tip of the iceberg, and reviewing Google's best practices guidelines is of the utmost importance. Their free guidance covers everything from website tips to how to use advanced Analytic reports to monitor conversion. It provides nitty-gritty indicators marketers can use to better track Google performance.

Like it or not, the "global community" is upon us, so it's time to understand how to leverage your "Made to Market" community.

Social Tracking

In the fall of 2020, new research revealed that marketing leaders claim cross-platform analytics are key to long-term success. Currently, analytics tools only offer isolated snapshots of individual platforms, a completely interconnected story is still missing. As we've seen, powerful tools are available to analyze our social media performance and equally powerful tools to analyze our web presence. Seasoned marketers understand that data is critical to sound business decisions. As marketers around the globe respond to changes in consumer behavior brought on by digital shifts, consumer attention, and even COVID-19, leveraging data is crucial to maintain customer loyalty and drive new revenue streams. However, few readily available tools tell marketers how both work together to accomplish connected business benchmarks. Thus, the next area of uncertainty that marketers must plan to master—myself included—is upon us and requires attention.

For now, savvy marketers can implement social tracking mechanisms to uncover key elements that tie cross-platform analytics. Knowing how, when, where, what, and why to post on your social media accounts can be overwhelming, especially when you don't have a lot of time.

The solution is a basic trick—not something I invented (totally wish I did, it's mad genius)—that I've implemented to achieve increased organic engagement rates. I put the theory to practice six years ago, and it's proven its power in spades to track social content strategies ever since.

The key is reverse-engineering the social tracking process by engaging the 70% + 20% + 10% rule, a content creation ratio strategy. With it, marketers can determine a baseline for communication and use it to listen and elicit conversations around shared values and thinking in an open environment far away from the manipulative feelings that a sales-focused message can conjure.

So, I'd like to dive a bit deeper and spell out how these percentages work together to build your web marketing strategy. This infographic was cleverly developed by Crystal Vilkaitis, owner of CrystalMedia, who has visually defined the 70/20/10 Social Posting Rule, as seen on the following page.

70% Custom Branded Stories
20% Industry related shares
10% Sales posts

I've applied this rule across all the platforms I use, and it has unfailingly steered me in the direction of increased organic engagement. The following steps will help you understand the hustle that goes into creating a posting calendar that aligns with the content strategy we've already discussed.

70/20/10 SOCIAL POSTING RULE

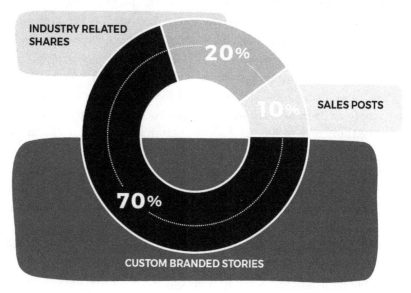

Adapted from Crystal Vilkaitis,
Owner of CrystalMedia

Step 1. Understanding how the rule breaks down

Let's apply this rule for posting 10 times in 1 week:

70% = 7 **Branding** posts
20% = 2 **Industry Related** posts
10% = 1 **Sales** post

Branding posts are original content in the platform's native language. Yes, your delivery should change from platform to platform. You shouldn't post the same exact message across all platforms.

The **industry-related** post is not just any share but shares from others in your related field that also have AMAZING content. Don't forget to alert them, and hopefully, they'll join the conversation and share some love in return.

And then there was one. Yes, it's recommended to post no more than one **sales** post per week for all 7 days. So, make it good! Wondering how? Continue reading. I go into this in more detail below.

Step 2. Branding

70% of this rule is dedicated to brand awareness. This is original content that speaks directly to your specific clientele in your organic voice. This is the fun part! I'm encouraging you to be yourself here. Live it, own it, and watch your followers fall in love with it! Stop trying to mimic another successful brand in your industry. Be your own brand. When you spend time doing what comes naturally, rather than learning how to be something else and then struggling to replicate it, a lot of extra time opens up. Watch our stories at @TrailTherapyAL to see what I mean.

So, this branding content is new, or a version of some larger piece of original content like we discussed using in the Gary Vaynerchuk example. When I say "original," I mean something that hasn't been done and that you can't find anywhere else on the internet.

This is **not** where you share links or do any kind of promotion. This is where you build the personality behind your brand that leads to consumer trust and long-term, profitable relationships. This is where you showcase what makes you, you!

I get that it's tough to find a balance for your brand's voice, but testing makes that possible. The video by Marie Forleo titled *Great Branding You Can Smell From Miles Away* will help you determine how to put your real personality in your brand while unapologetically doing so. In it, you'll "learn three brilliant branding strategies that Poo Pourri uses to cause a real stink in the marketplace."

In short, the smart strategies she covers are easy to incorporate.

1. "Know Your Poo-crew."
We've already established if you're talking to everyone, you're talking to no one! From their visual assets to their copy, Poo Pourri certainly doesn't. They maintain hyper-focused on their target persona, the glamor-appreciating young woman who thinks poop is hilarious! Watch their communication tactics to see they never waiver from this one woman. Yes, they have products for all, but they rely on her to spread the word and build their brand on their behalf.

2. "Don't give a crap about everybody else!"
Poo Pourri is not concerned or moved by the naysayers who are offended by their brand strategy. In fact, their bold branding purposely repulses those who are not

their target customer. Their singular focus is to communicate with and delight this one gal, and they are wildly successful as a result.

"If you want a fresh brand, don't give a crap about someone who thinks you stink!" @MarieForleo

3. Spray your brand's scent everywhere!

Consider every corner where your brand content is placed is paramount to the content creation and results tracking correlation. Yes, that even includes brand development for your FAQ, 404 redirects and website "thank you" pages. These pages tend to be the ones that need to be tracked most, as they're typically the exit step of a web visit. These pages provide a powerful, often untouched, opportunity to make an impression, which may be the difference between gaining and losing a customer.

Once you've researched your way into a confident brand voice that works best for your target customers, play with it, track it, and analyze the results. Managing your online presence means constantly tweaking, adjusting, and changing what works for your customers.

Step 3. Curating the right "industry related" shares

This is where you find and share what's going on in the world your customer cares most about. However, 20% of your shares should stay on point. Yes, you can get fun, creative, and even a bit crazy here if that's where your customer and brand aligns. But the same message should be found throughout each of your choices. If you're a beauty company, your shares should be about beauty. This could include an at-home YouTube video on how (not) to curl your hair because, oh yeah, it burns easy.

Yes, that really happened! Search it and see!

To that same beauty company, don't share a trending animal video just because it's currently viral, and you want the views. Can I say it? I think I will...tacky! You are busting your butt to keep a clean, fresh aroma about your brand, don't make it easy for your clients to choke on an overcast odor.

Step 4. The Sales Pitch

Ah, sales! Last but certainly not least, sales posts should only make up one-tenth of what you share online! Shocking, right?!?! And marketing should check with sales to inquire what that looks like on a weekly basis. With only 10% of your shares being shameless "sales" promotions, it's important to make these count. But don't think that's a green light to go off-message from your other 9 posts. Your promo should feel, sound, and taste just as seamless as the rest of the week's posts. It should not cause skid marks in their feed requiring consumers to slam on their brakes in frustration. If you've been successful with your branding, sharing your sales pitch should not interrupt any other message.

I'm not going to reinvent the wheel here because Gary Vaynerchuk explains the art of how to land your sales pitch perfectly every time in his book *Jab, Jab, Jab, Right Hook.*

You don't always have to be selling if 70% of your posts ROCK!

Applying this content strategy solidifies the social tracking process. When you know the types of content you are creating, measured against the engagement of each, it becomes clear which *message type and timing* is most effective. As a result, it draws clear and concise conclusions around your next best steps. Now you can professionally and confidently express your reasoning behind marketing decisions that lead your organization to be "Made to Market" ready!

NOTES

Chapter 10

BUILD IT, OR THEY WILL NEVER COME

Brand & Beyond

For anyone who's been in marketing for a while, I know I'm not about to tell you anything new. Still, it demands repeating for the sake of establishing truth-based marketing practices. Your brand is not just a logo, and a new logo is not the solution to your branding problems. Statistically, the more emotion a brand conjures, the more money consumers spend.

Take Nike, for example. Their logo, the "swoosh," isn't what made them into who they are today. It was the deep emotion that Nike consistently elicited over time.

The very first Nike commercial was launched in 1988. It shows 80-year-old Walt Stack recounting his story about running seventeen miles every morning, even in the winter. The one question Mr. Stack was often asked, was "how do you keep your teeth from chattering in the wintertime?" His response, "I leave them in my locker."

"Just do it" is not a swoosh. "Just do it" is a declaration that, "no matter what, I will!"

Again, in 2012, we see the same message geared toward a completely different generation.

In a more modern branded commercial, we see, "find your greatness." Almost thirty years later, this iconic brand still hasn't deviated from telling its consistent brand messaging. "No matter what, I will" has stirred emotions in people across the globe, across socioeconomic status, across cultural divides who all feel they can accomplish more with Nike.

That's branding. It goes WAY beyond a logo to tell a story that relates to the individual.

Branding is an experience.

It's what people say about you when you're not in the room.

It's the feeling that lingers after an interaction with you.

It's the first impression someone gets driving up to your brick-and-mortar location before ever stepping foot in the door.

It's the result of consistent brand marketing communications.

Voice is your brand's personality—and it's always the same. Your voice is the unique way you present your brand to the world. It's your personality, the type of language you use, and the way you use that language. Given voice is your personality, tone is how you express that personality, and tone varies with context. Every piece of content reflects your brand. So, your content must intentionally and thoughtfully maintain a consistent voice to see Nike-like results.

Back in my Avant Creative heyday, we became experts at accomplishing all the above as a team. Using smart tools, innovative communication strategies, and modern consumer insights, we built socially connected user experiences that created brand loyalty and marketing solutions to make the most of our client's brand potential.

Marketers should implement several intentional actions during the brand development process, and I'll show you what that looks like soon. But first, consider an example of how branding without an effective process in place can spur catastrophic results.

Take the recent Oak Park Illinois rebrand case, an example of brand development that makes marketers want to run and hide. Nothing says, "Welcome Home!" like a phallic-shaped municipal logo, right? No! The phallic presentation was initially part of a tourism push for the western suburb, intended to give the impression that Oak Park residents are risk-takers. But anyone who sees this tubular rendering—and its step out of line "strapline" (no joke)—probably isn't thinking about skydiving. These are the kinds of brand risks that will certainly not end in the generational longevity that brands such as Nike has achieved.

At Avant, we avoided making such colossal brand mistakes as we built brands for the long haul rather than a publicity stunt. I was thrilled to work with such a talented team that created powerful brands from scratch. Our team was a dynamic balance of dreamers and doers who believed in relentlessly exploring what's possible. We were passionate, playful, and deeply invested in each design piece that ended up on display for the world to see. We had the skill, knowledge, and creativity to visualize brand concepts from a few scattered seeds. We often asked clients to send us Pinterest boards, color swatches, and layout designs to provide visual cues to accompany their descriptive overlays. We then created interconnected communications and conducted target market research. Only then were we able to define, design, and combine a foundational design standard better known as the "style guide" or "brand kit," which set the foundational principles for a brand to build upon.

We had the pleasure of working with various industries—from tech to food—and crafted designs for over sixty brands which contributed to improved market share for many of our clients. Our work created simply defined, authentic, memorable, and consistent brand foundations designed to stand the test of time. Of course, none of this was possible without the graphic design capabilities that Merrilee brought to the team, as we obsessed over exceeding expectations, consistently going above and beyond with our research, technical talents, and visionary direction.

Finding Your Voice

In the search to articulate your brand, do not ask, "What's our brand?" The question instead is, "What's our story and why?" Logos aren't passed around to define who we are; they exist to accompany a good story.

A company's brand is a constant force that guides its customer messaging and reflects how the company sees itself engaging in the world. Cohesive design and consistent voice provide subtle reminders to form a connection, while specific campaign structures evoke a direct response. The brand is platform-agnostic—it doesn't matter where it shows up—and its constant focus serves as a visual reminder to engage and participate.

A business's voice should reflect its customer's voice: a collective of customer expectations. Merrilee said it best, herself, in a 2016 article she wrote about the three P's — **promises, perception, and persuasion.**

This section teaches you how these three P's work together so you can stand apart.

PROMISE: Communication centers on the brand's promise.

What goes through your mind every time you see Starbucks? The promise of a smooth, creamy latte or rich, fragrant coffee in a peaceful yet communal remote work environment. How about Netflix? The promise of escape through stories in the comfort of your own home, in your own bed, and never having to stray far from your sleeved blanket, the Snuggie.

A brand indicates a promise to provide the services/product the customer deserves. And delivering on that promise over time is what creates trust in the business. Maybe it's the fact that the organization provides something unique that's difficult to get elsewhere. Perhaps a company promotes social responsibility and gives back to the community. Or maybe an organization helps people succeed by providing resources that save time and money.

Whatever the promise, it's a marketer's job to communicate it to the intended audience.

PERCEPTION: How people view and connect with a business.

Perception mirrors the brand, so the message and meaning should mimic the company's true vision. Its target market should resonate with the visual, vocal, and vibe of the branding. For example, cool colors promote peace and tranquility, while bright colors create a sense of fun and excitement. Photographs that promote action and movement paired with bright colors resonate with an active, energetic, and determined audience. A message of exploration and discovery will enhance a company's mission.

Perception is what you see at first glance. This includes the company's visual identity like logo and color palette, photography, slogan or tagline, and overall look and feel. It's how customers see your organization based on all the seen and unseen cues that are built around your voice.

PERSUASION: Marketing uses a brand message that engages.

Persuasion isn't meant to be a lie. It's a compelling truth that focuses on what the audience already knows about the brand. A persuasive message is convincing, direct, and easy to interpret. **It always provides value when offering services or products.** An expert marketer can position a persuasive message that highlights the company's expertise, instilling a sense of comfort and confidence, while delivering precise messaging to a seeking audience. That's why blogs and social media have become increasingly important for businesses and organizations.

Marketing should be used with multiple media vehicles such as print, web, and social media. This includes everything from printed collateral to websites and apps because they articulate the tangible touchpoints that visually signify persuasive capabilities.

Making Your Mark

A style guide is a core brand asset that maintains the brand voice and visual acuity customers come to know and respect. Organizations and marketers frequently struggle with inconsistent branding. It may be because they don't have a foundational visual identity in the form of a brand kit to maintain much-needed consistency.

Initial development and maintenance of a brand kit are how great brands stand out and get noticed. Protecting and monitoring the use of branding elements is key. Each piece of content produced by a brand is a vital customer touchpoint. Visually inconsistent touchpoints play a significant role in diluting a message and creating confusion over time. The brand kit or style guide ensures unified consistency during the design process, so when people search and discover the organization, they encounter the same look and feel each and every time.

Consider the case when employers assign social management marketing to the youngest employee. *They're on it all the time, so they must know how to use it,* right?!

For a visual clue of what I'm explaining, head over to Instagram and scroll through the @shakeshack feed. Not just a couple of scrolls, I mean really scroll!

What does it feel like? Playful, vibrant, humor with no brand deviation at all.

Now head over to @houstonrockets and scroll for a bit, then tell me if the same clearly defined emotions are elicited. There are a few, but none as clearly brand-centric as @shakeshack, @tjmax, @takearecess, @madewell, and my personal favorite @gopro. All maintain consistent brand feels, which tell the story of the customer's experience, no matter how far back you scroll. Most likely because they didn't assign the youngest employee to the helm.

Your company's brand kit provides visual guidelines for content creation across all communication platforms, and marketing professionals know how and why to uphold these standards. From social content to business cards, the brand kit sets the design parameters to ensure brand consistency. In most cases, the brand kit is added to a website for direct access by designers, eliminating the need for new design elements made from scratch.

Clearly defined organizational missions, goals, and values allow marketers to structure brand strategies that are effective, cohesive, and truly remarkable. When used consistently across all platforms and media vehicles, your representation begins to foster relationships with clients and the public. Your increased visibility leads to further memorability, awareness, and equity.

A well-constructed style guide assigns a personal identity to a brand, making it progressively recognizable, situating the organization for success.

Once a foundational brand identity is created, you can apply that brand and its values to *any* visual element to maximize business promotion potential. A brand must be recognizable to develop loyalty and build trust, and a brand kit is one of the first foundational steps to ensure that happens.

Ready to get your brand "Made to Market" ready?

Start by downloading the brand development playbook on www.Avant-Creative.com. In it, you'll learn about the essential brand elements that many businesses have yet to implement.

NOTES

Chapter 11

THE DARWINISM OF DESIGN

Professionally, I'm not quite what I once was with Merrilee. So, during the research process for this book, I was delighted to discover two articles she wrote to help me better articulate the vital nuances of branding. One played an assist in the previous chapter, while the other deserves a chapter all to itself. The following article is Merrilee's original work and thought process behind the delicate balance between the science, psychology, and art of the brand-building process.

The Darwinism of Design – By Merrilee Hale, Creative Director

Good design answers questions, while great design also solves problems.

Trends shift, technology advances, but the cornerstone of design is found in science—not subjectivity.

The human brain processes visual information 60,000 times faster than verbal or written information, and visual information is more easily recalled. That's because visual stimuli are inherently spatial, while auditory stimuli are sequential; it requires far more of our brain's resources to recall something we've heard or read versus something we've seen.

We're consistently taking in complex visual data, which also sparks our inner dialogue. The information is stored twice: once in visual code and once in auditory code. This increases the chances of recalling visual information with proper context and accuracy.

As English speakers, we read from top to bottom and left to right, so it makes sense to position graphics and images that lead us to specific information in the same way, promoting retention. After three days, most people can only recall 10% of the information they've read, where if paired with a relevant image, 10% jumps to 65%. That's one reason we often see a logo on a website at the top left instead of the bottom right or even the top right. We want our customers to recall our logo, the visual representation of our company, and position it in a memorable way that is seen as often as possible. This is also the logic behind why most websites have trended toward developing a static top menu even when scrolling to the bottom of a page.

Positioning images, graphics, and colors effectively draws the eye and emphasizes specific content that you want to make more memorable. This is particularly effective when referencing services provided or advantages in choosing your company. Repetition of colors, fonts, paragraph styling, icons, and images allows us to make valuable connections to a brand. This must be presented in a consistent, cohesive way across all media platforms and vehicles. In design, form follows function. Every piece of data, requirement, specification, and representation is just a small piece of the overarching puzzle determining how information is presented and organized.

Creating logos with room for adjustment based on size and space provides versatility, while branding kits and style guides dictate how and where images, colors, and text styles should be used.

Print and web media should maintain similar styling aspects as much as possible to improve recall and recognition, which increases a brand's credibility and trust. But the science of design isn't just about hard evidence; it's also about the context of nuanced perception such as psychology and emotion.

Psychographics, for example, is the study, classification, and market industry research of people according to behaviors, attitudes, aspirations, personality, values, and psychology. This also affects how color influences emotion, forms connections to experiences, and shapes our internal view—and if those sound familiar, it's because these are elements that determine consumer behavior—often identifying the "why" of how and when people buy. Remember, demographics merely explain who the buyer is.

Yes, data is important, but the information is limited; it doesn't explain potential customer interests, attitudes, or motivations—which is where psychographics steps in.

Color and visual appearance substantially impact consumer behavior and contribute to 93% of a buying decision. The jury is out on colors evoking hyperspecific emotions, as there is an interplay between categorical information like age, gender, education, upbringing, experiences, and values. Our general associations with colors, however, are evidence-based, so if design adjustments are in the future of your brand, you should consider the following signifying traits:

Red: Excitement, youth, strength, friendliness
Orange: Friendliness, cheerfulness, confidence, power, forward-thinking
Yellow: Optimism, clarity, warmth, compassion
Green: Peace, growth, health, calm, nature/conservation
Blue: Trust, dependability, strength, tranquility, loyalty, competence
Purple: Creativity, imagination, wisdom, royalty
Pink: Charming, sentimental, feminine
Black: Strength, power, independence, security
Brown: Ruggedness, nature/conservation
Gray: Balance, neutrality, calm
Silver: Elegance, glamor, fashionable
Gold: Dominance, royalty, wealth

While certain colors' signifying traits can be used appropriately, it all hinges on your target audience. Gold may win over an account with white-collar professionals who want to be seen as industry leaders who afford lavish lifestyles. Whereas blue-collar workers who resent the idea of royalty and luxury and those who don't get their hands dirty, gold may lose their support. A brand is more than the visual identity representing an overall approach to design, so understanding basic science on how we see and perceive can help build a better approach to design.

In life, we quickly learn the need to adapt—on multiple levels—and part of Darwinism is the ability to adapt to change. For field marketers, we can see changes coming and are actively working to make sense of them and adjust for the future.

Technology is advancing at an unprecedented rate, an engine fueled by demand, cost management, advancing processes, and efficiency.

We continue to see the market trend toward flourishing large corporations while small businesses struggle for solvency.

What's a small business to do?

Well, they offer lower, value-added pricing and quality products to survive but miss out on opportunities that could place them ahead of the competition.

If a business has existed for half a decade or more, consider the various parts of the operation: iterations of software programs, process management and efficiency protocols, equipment, and material upgrades.

In an age of evolving markets and digital communication, word-of-mouth referrals and postcard mailings alone are not an effective form of lead generation. Without an effective and all-encompassing web presence, an organization may lose potential clients faster than it realizes. Combining a dynamic, responsive website with social media marketing and a refreshed branding approach can do wonders for a business's image and reach, regardless of its size.

According to a Pitney Bowes survey, 76% of small businesses say their ideal marketing strategy encompasses a combination of both print and digital communication. More than half of Nielsen survey respondents said they used a social media advertising campaign in conjunction with print media.

Performing a quick search on the web for "local printing companies," I found 112,000,000 results with over ten paginations. At the top of the list were three advertisements for online-only printers, along with four franchises listed below. Without a website containing SEO (search engine optimization), a small business will likely land far down the list. HubSpot reports that 75% of users never scroll past the first page of search results, which doesn't bode well for many companies. Take a look at these staggering statistics regarding online presence, polished design, and functionality:

- 48% of users say that if they arrive on a business site that isn't working well on mobile, they take it as an indication of the business simply not caring. (Source: MarginMedia)

- 40% of people will abandon a web page if it takes more than *three seconds* to load. (Source: Econsultancy)

- $1.1 trillion of all retail sales in 2011 were "web-influenced." (Source: Forrester Research)

- 66% of small businesses are maintaining or increasing spend on digital marketing. (AT&T Small Business Technology Poll)

- 72% of consumers trust online reviews as much as personal recommendations from real people. (Search Engine Land)

- 82% of small business owners said their main source of new business is referrals. (Constant Contact)

- 69% of consumers are more likely to use a local business if it has information on a social media site. (comScore Networks and TMP Directional Marketing)

- 49% of sites fail to comply with basic usability principles, and 50% of online sales are lost because visitors can't find content. (Forrester)

- 88% of consumers search for a type of local business on a mobile device call or go to that business within 24 hours. (Google Mobile Movement Study)

The statistics above are compelling and call for action; they all demonstrate that businesses require a dynamic, responsive website that:

- works on different platforms and devices;

- provides relevant, current information on services and products;

- and offers value-added services specific to the industry—think file uploads and accurate quote generation.

The internet has been around for far longer than we realize. Websites gained greater popularity in the early 1990s. Get this—Apple first launched their website in 1987, while Google launched in 1994!

See what I mean?

All of the searchable content from this era can't be erased entirely. Still, search engines like Google are making it more difficult to come across information that hasn't been updated in, say, 20 years, with their newest ranking signal that launched in April (2021).

Even if you created your website 2, 5, or 10 years ago and have just made minor updates to it, Google will dock your ranking based on the following factors:

- Mobile-friendly (dynamic, responsive) vs. Static: If loading your website on a smartphone forces you to zoom in to see content, or images and other content are broken or improperly shifted, your website is not "mobile-friendly." Google will send traffic to competitors who do maintain a mobile-friendly presence.

- Static vs. Dynamic Content: If your website hasn't been updated in months or years, Google thinks your content is outdated and will drive traffic to similar industry sites with newer postings.

- Outdated media content: As of September 1 (2021), the Google Chrome browser will block Flash by default because of persistent security issues in Adobe's flagship media streaming technology. Other browsers are bound to follow Google's lead, supporting newer formats available in HTML 5.

- Slow loading pages: If your website is slow, ensure proper compression of images and files, upgrade to a better hosting plan, or move your website to its own virtual private server (or VPS).

- Unloadable content: Broken links, unplayable content, faulty redirects, app download interstitials, and irrelevant cross-links are ultimately bad for business.

You can fix several of the above issues by resizing photographs or digital images and updating broken links. If your site is unresponsive or loads slowly, you may want to think about how you or your developer built the site—if you heavily relied on Flash, now may be the time to rethink your strategy. Flash development has ceased, but you can integrate the same techniques using different methods far more appropriate and cause less bandwidth usage—performing at fast speeds even on 4G networked mobile devices.

Consider the Darwinism of Design as the survival of the fittest for businesses that continue to evolve based on the current market emerging toward well-designed communication and technological trends. Those who don't follow suit will be left behind, creating favorable conditions for companies that understand the importance of a dynamic and current web presence.

NOTES

Chapter 12

BUILDING AN ENGAGED SOCIAL AUDIENCE

Branding is a vehicle used by marketers to reflect not only what the organization offers its audience, but it can also represent the organization's values or culture. That's why it's essential to understand how consumers perceive the organization through its branding.

But how can you possibly know what customers are thinking?

Apply social tools to better understand behavior—a manifestation of internal dialogue—to build and engage an audience in a way that exposes their point of view of your brand. While social media is a fantastic way to make others aware of your organization, it's only a single part of a larger marketing process.

A marketer's job is to bridge the gap between follower awareness and fan engagement. It's about consistent communication over time. The hard fact is audience-building doesn't happen immediately. Although capturing explosive growth sounds tempting, it's not a strategy, and if you plan to do this right, there are no cheat codes. Gaining fan engagement is normally a gradual process—not a one and done—gaining momentum over time with the right processes in place. So, let's discuss tools, tactics, and best practices to build a highly engaged audience, leaning into consistent growth.

The Why of Content Creation

So far, we've addressed the "how-to" of content creation, but we haven't yet discussed the "why," the purpose of content creation and its role in the overall digital marketing strategy. So, let's do that now.

Over the past few years, an unnerving trend in business caused me to stop and focus on the effect of content creation on a marketing strategy. I call it, "Pepper Posting," which is throwing up some random post here and there to satisfy a perceived requirement to do so. But there's no real direction or explanation for why this strategy was used other than, "I know I need to post, so I just put whatever pops into my head that day."

It's no surprise that companies everywhere realize their need to transition their efforts to include digital, but I discovered they're still confused as to why. This became apparent in the "2020 Social Media Marketing Industry Report" from *Social Media Examiner*, which states that 89% of marketers want to know what the best social media marketing strategies are.

You'll have a better idea of how to make that happen by the end of this chapter.

Businesses tend to open a social account (or four), link their accounts from their website, post mostly the same sales-focused content messages across all chosen platforms for about three months and then give up because they don't see the results they hoped for. When asked, "What were the results you hoped for?" the answer is "More sales, of course!" Um. That's not a strategy. A goal, yes, possibly a wish. But social media is not a business genie. Rubbing the Facebook lamp and walking away before your goal is realized is not a sound business tactic.

In all my research on social practitioners and content creation, I've encountered this common trend with almost every client. "Social media" is not a machine for plugging in a formula and spitting out the results you want. But, at the risk of sounding cliché, online business interactions need to be social! Why? Because people use the internet for their vetting process. So, long before a business starts a social account (and posts any old content), the audience must be considered.

Sounds like a no-brainer, right?

It baffles me that businesses seeking likes, shares, and, sometimes fan purchases frequently forget about the people behind those interactions and often don't consider them during the content creation process.

How is that even possible?

Smart marketers actually look at it from a different point of view: How do you create a loyal, locked-in community of consumers who are:

- brand advocates committed to your cause;

- unshakable, supportive, and dedicated loyalists;

- individuals who believe in what your organization stands for, not just static products or services?

As consumers appear to become less loyal, brands must re-imagine loyalty thinking, starting with those accused of being least loyal — millennials. As a millennial myself, I always give a good eye-roll around this statistic. Often dubbed flakey or hard to please, the reality is we're just really good at knowing when someone is lying to us. We don't trust much, and we believe even less of what's being "sold" to us. Think about it. A large chunk of us where becoming adults as the September 11, 2001 tragedy took place, and we still aren't sure who's to blame. So, when a lack of honesty in the marketplace emerges, you better believe we'll jump ship when we feel the wool is pulled over our eyes. The reality is, over 60% of millennials stated they are reasonably dedicated to purchasing only quality products from **trusted brands**.

But who do millennials trust? Brands are making it harder, not easier, to overcome our critical thinking.

I used a popular whitening toothpaste off and on for several years. Believing the brand messaging—and ultimate whitening promise—I trusted that it would just take some time to see the results. In five years, do you think I ever saw whiter teeth? Nope! During that time, I tried multiple promises of whiter teeth with no real results. Defaulting to the popular brand every time, mostly because that sparkling-white packaging wooed me at eye level while I stood contemplating in the aisle. Finally, it hit me. This promise is not true.

So, I switched to Arm and Hammer baking soda. Why? Because they offer no fluff. Its toothpaste using ingredients I trusted to touch my skin. That's it. Fresh breath, job done. Now I've been using it for close to five years, not because of the hype but the lack thereof. Millennials aren't brand flakes because they can't be pleased; they are brand flakes because once they figure out they've been lied to—whether in five years or five minutes—they jump ship and never look back.

So, this idea of shaming customers because they don't purchase goods at the volume their parents did, ain't gonna work moving forward. That's a lot of energy to waste when lost sales are ever increasing in this category. Always be truthful when communicating with customers, don't forget to listen, and adjust to their feedback.

What the old methodology on building brand loyalty missed—and is now better understood—is the need to win hearts and minds. The new consumer is not a mass consumer. Today's consumer should be engaged through a community of consumers and treated at an individual level. Moving forward, crowdsourcing marketing models will drive brand loyalty as a powerful communication outlet.

A great example of forward-thinking crowdsourcing marketing includes LEGO. By establishing the LEGO Ideas platform, users can submit their ideas for new LEGO sets. Consumers are also able to vote and offer feedback on submitted ideas. LEGO reviews any idea that receives over 10,000 votes. If a submitter's idea is selected, they get to work with the LEGO team to make the idea a reality and even receive royalties on design project sales. The platform not only supports new idea generation but also validates LEGO's demand for such ideas. One of the most successful crowdsourcing sets to date is the Beatles' "Yellow Submarine" set.

In today's turbulent world, people are hungry for a sense of connection; and in lean economic times, every company needs new ways to do more with what it already has. Unfortunately, although many organizations work to build customer loyalty, marketing efficiency, and brand authenticity that strong communities deliver, few understand what it takes to achieve benefits from each. Worse, most subscribe to serious misconceptions about what brand communities are and how the community think-tank model works.

The brand's community does not exist to serve the business. The community exists to better serve the customers within it. This idea of community-driven business development builds upon the foundational pieces to create brand loyalty and buy-in.

I'm not one to say, "just do this one trick for maximum results." There are just too many unique community complexities to apply a one-size-fits-all marketing strategy. The one exception that I will continue to share until it's no longer relevant is the 70/20/10 ratio rule discussed in more detail earlier. When you have to start building a community from scratch, applying this rule elicits community conversations. It's a perfect content-building link between brand interaction and asking for the sale. Yes, there are times to ask for the sale. Those times just shouldn't dominate your online content strategy. Again, when broken down, the percentage of content shared looks like this:

70% Custom Branded Stories.
20% Industry-related Shares.
10% Sales Posts.

As a result of following the 70/20/10 rule, increased organic engagement and authentic customer communication will be achieved!

It is possible to create content that trains a community to market for you.

How do I know there's a breakdown in traditional marketing methods? By evaluating organizational engagement rates, which I consider a baseline. Just like when you go to the doctor, and your vitals are measured against your previous visits, serving as your baseline health status. It's the very first metric the nurse checks upon arrival. The same holds true in marketing with engagement rates.

Let's look at a quick example with the company Entrepreneur. With over 3 million followers, you'd think their engagement rates would be incredibly high. Not the case. In a recent post I calculated an average of **.49%** engagement.

In comparison, a small Chamber of Commerce in Alabama with less than 10,000 followers achieved an average of 20% engagement per post.

But there's opportunity and plenty of room for the Entrepreneur brand to grow their engagement, brand presence, and, ultimately, dollars spent with their organization.

The first place to look — hashtags! There's a tremendous amount of activity around the hashtag #Entrepreneur. On Twitter, we see immeasurable conversations with new posts taking place every minute. And on Instagram, over 200,000 conversations took place under the same hashtag. So clearly, the engagement potential is there.

But where is the disconnect?

A serious lack of content-focused consumer connections.

You know the saying, "If it ain't broke, don't fix it?" My take on that is, "If it seems broke, let's fix it."

What we now see is traditional marketing tactics are swiftly decreasing in effectiveness because consumers are growing savvier, require more transparency, and want to know who the organization is—in full. While marketers seem stuck applying antiquated tactics.

NOTES

_____

_____

_____

_____

_____

_____

_____

_____

_____

_____

_____

_____

_____

_____

_____

_____

_____

Chapter 13

RELATIONSHIP MARKETING: EVEN THE WRINKLES? ESPECIALLY THE WRINKLES!

Businesses are so busy trying to catch up with what a marketing strategy even looks like, they're missing the next significant shift: relationship marketing. This phenomenon involves sharing the process, not merely shifting the packaging around. That means full integration of business process documentation and its effect on consumers by considering who we are and what we bring to the relationship at all levels.

Consumers are desperate for businesses to rip through the pretty packaging and reveal what's inside, whether it's as shiny as the other guy's or not. If the business's offering truly fills a need, consumers will embrace it. Then telling that story through the consumer experience creates the disruptive breakthrough that leads to long-term success.

Alright, so how do you know your content creation strategy is building the right relationships?

So far, we've discussed measuring social success, including how to build and analyze content engagement using the 70/20/10 rule. But there's another way to measure the effectiveness of your content health, which goes beyond social media. It involves taking a deep dive under the hood of your website for an in-depth, raw look at what's going on.

Here are 4 ways to measure the effectiveness of your current content.

1. Site content drill-down

At the bottom of the behavior tab in your Google Analytics platform, you'll find the label called "site content." The drill-down tab is where you'll find your best-performing pages ranked from "highest" to "least high" website traffic performance.

Think of content drill-down as a high-level view of the organization's content and visitor-ranked content based on page popularity. Use this report to analyze the topics that draw folks from social media to determine future content creation ideas based on increased topic interest.

The good news is top-ranked tools like Parse.ly, Alteryx, HubSpot, Moz, and Adobe Analytics are developing features that enable marketers to link all digital marketing platforms through one analytics account. Unfortunately, many marketers don't have the budget or the staff to take on such a tool. However, creative alternatives found in Google Analytics can help draw lines of correlation that lead to meaningful action steps.

2. MONITOR "Behavior Flow."

The Google Analytics "behavior" tab is where you'll discover insight on the thought process of page selection throughout your site. This report reveals which pages were served up to pair visitors with the relevant topic they searched. Here, you'll gain insight into the content topic that finally led them not only onto your site but off the site as well. The value in this report is determining the blog articles that worked and the ones that flopped. Armed with that information, you can now improve future content planning.

Sometimes, for whatever reason, the social content created to drive awareness to a compelling article doesn't mesh with the social community. But that doesn't mean we just chop out that piece of content and throw it away. We use it to identify the correlation between social and web content cohesiveness. This also helps shed light on what is and isn't working in the customer conversion process, which is all part of painting the customer behavior picture to make better strategically grounded decisions.

Under the "acquisition" tab, click on "social," then "network referrals." You'll see a clear breakdown identifying social platforms responsible for sending web visitors to specific content. You'll see the content that produced the most web visits from social traffic. If the content flow is not aligned with popular social traffic referrals, it's safe to say there's a disconnect between consistent brand presentation flow in your overall web presence.

For example, when I look at my website's social acquisition page, I see that LinkedIn is responsible for converting more social network referrals than any other platform. Armed with that information, it becomes clear where my web content is mainly being consumed. With that, I'll develop a more streamlined LinkedIn content strategy.

3. SET UP "Goals."

Google Goals is the most delightful tracking mechanism ever invented! Although we talked about them already in this book, I wanted to tackle them again because they are oh-so-very important!

I don't care what your stance is on using Google Analytics; this one will delight even the most frustrated naysayer. You'll find goals under the "conversions" tab on the right-hand side of your analytics dashboard. Unlike most analytics reports that come pre-filled based on previously gathered data, you must set up your goal first. So, if you're visiting this report page for the first time, there will be no data to review.

I'll get into how to set up a goal in just a bit. But first, it's important to under-stand the validity of its use as a tracking mechanism. Remember my very first marketing contract with INCARE Technologies and the career-changing ques-tion? "Sarah, how will you determine the ROI of this marketing campaign?" A question you most likely have been asked. A question every organization should be asking marketers. My quest for an answer led me to set up a Google Goal, which catapulted me toward a solution.

This is where you get to determine whether your website is performing to the metrics you deemed important, key performance metrics that are already estab-lished.

Is it important that someone sign up to schedule a free 15-minute Zoom call with you? Set up a goal to track it.

Is it important that you know how many people landed on a 404 error page? Set up a goal to track it.

Is it important that you know how many people downloaded your free pocket guide and where they're located? Set up a goal to track it.

See, Google Analytics is really good at serving up data covering every aspect of online traffic from country origin to the user device to what keywords they typed in the search bar to find you. While important, those are not essential metrics to every business. Each organization has its own unique key performance indicators and tracking them is vital to making decisions. Here is where marketers can prove themselves invaluable at serving up precise information on questions your leadership is looking to answer. Use this free tool to your advantage and finally get to the bottom of what others are still scratching their heads to figure out.

As explained earlier, this was one of the first tracking mechanisms I learned as a marketer. I understood early on just how important it was to drill down to very personalized touchpoints with a specific customer base. Goals get granular in ways you'd never imagine, so the question is, what's important for you to track? This is where you'll be able to track personalized goals to make data-driven decisions.

You could easily google "how to set up a google goal" and end with quite a few easy-to-follow instructions. But to buttress this task, I'll provide a brief overview.

- On the bottom of the left-hand side of your analytics dashboard, you'll find the "admin" tab. Here you'll see columns.

- Under column three on the far right, you'll find the "goals" tab under the title "all website data."

- Click the "new goal" button and begin setting up to 20 specific benchmarks that lead to tracking the important visitor accomplishments on your website.

4. Acquisition Referrals.

Under the "traffic" tab in Google Analytics, you'll have the opportunity to better understand the percentage of visitors that make it to your website after visiting your social pages. Now, for many sites I manage and monitor, social traffic is at the top of the list for referral traffic.

Monitoring these markers and syncing with Agorapulse provides measurable content performance. We now know that content makes up the pillar pieces of a marketing strategy. So, measuring content performance informs how to build out the pieces of your strategy. To truly reach a broader audience and appeal to various demographics, it's not enough to just offer a lot of content. You need to provide various forms of it that work together to tell a whole story. This is called "content stacking."

Content stacking is the process of creating different pieces of content across various mediums. These are based on a larger piece, like a white paper, blog post, or even video. You can use the smaller pieces of content on different marketing channels, like social media, your blog, or your YouTube channel. By essentially "dissecting" your long-form content, you'll benefit from new content pieces that are fairly quick to create.

The point is, you've got to build the right content for customers to come, and when they get there, you must be able to track the efficacy of what you've built. As marketers, we tend to make our work very personal. But we must stop doing that. It's not about us and it's not always even about the organization. It's all about the customer!

NOTES

Chapter 14

MASS MARKETING MIX

Good Marketing Reaches People

'll never forget it. I was approaching a potential investor who'd just graduated with a Master in Business Administration (MBA) about the plausibility of a recently-invented product that was still in the ideation phase. He said, "Before I can back this, I must know your plan for the product's 4 P's."

I'm sorry, what now?

At that precise moment, my heart sank. How could we ever expect to move forward in business if graduate-level business majors cling to outdated theories behind launching a product?

The 4 P's of marketing he referred to—product, place, price, and promotion—was used to describe the marketing mix coined in the 1960s! Business school curricula still frequently include a discussion of the 4 P's of marketing. To this day, this outdated concept still pops up often in marketing books as a viable process model.

So, let's discuss why the 4 P's of marketing is a bygone theory so that as an evolved marketer or business owner, you can identify it, understand why it's antiquated, and progress to a more relevant model.

In a post-Covid world especially, the 4 P's foundational principles have all but lost their footing in a digital marketplace. What once were standards in the strategic marketing practice are all but blips on the face of a newly emerging radar. The 4 P's don't work for the online business world, a sector contributing $2.1 trillion to the U.S. economy, equating to 10.1% of U.S. GDP.

For marketing on the web, applying the traditional P's is a straight path to failure. The concepts force marketers into a paradigm that just isn't effective in a socially digital world. With a focus on everything except the customer, this previous-gen system needs a much-needed upgrade.

The sales-only focused funnel is out, and the customer life cycle is in. Say hello to the "5 A's:" awareness, advocate, appeal, ask, and act. It's simple, really. Its marketing mission is to improve customer service by continuously connecting with customers in creative, innovative ways to authentically develop lasting touchpoints. Why is this important? Because lasting touchpoints lead to loyalty.

The Five A's

Awareness. Exposure to the brand and the gateway to the customer journey.

Advocate. Active advocates spontaneously react to and recommend brands they love without being asked.

Appeal. The "wow" factor causes a brand to stand out from competitors. Moves from no knowledge to awareness.

Ask. The customer research process begins in an intentional way. Here the brand moves beyond peripheral awareness.

Act. The customer takes physical action to deepen the relationship, often a purchase.

THE 5 A'S

Adapted from Marketing 4.0, Philip Kotler, Hermawan Kartajaya, Iwan Setiawan

The cycle doesn't end with a brief celebration over sales, followed by moving on to a new customer. Modern-day customers are continuously in this cycle and must be treated as such. It's how good marketers reach people!

While some marketing models are passé, the foundations of marketing remain relevant as ever. These foundations serve as a compass to direct you to where you should apply the rules. The fault lies in blindly applying rules to every business situation. Marketing must consider the customer journey every step of the way to keep the organization on the path to success because true success comes from educating, informing, and entertaining people to be eager to do business with you.

So marketers, let's leave the four P's in the past where it belongs and embrace sincere connections with customers to achieve "Made to Market" readiness.

Building a social community as fresh as new socks

You know when you've just come home from a local boutique with a new pair of funky socks, and you couldn't be more excited? They are perfectly soft and snug on your feet and somehow even manage to add a little pep to your step. A few washes later, that pep starts to wane as the socks stretch, slouch, and, even worse, fade into dingy disarray. Before you know it, you've lost all but one mate, and you have to start the cycle all over again.

So disappointing!

But I've got good news. Building a highly responsive community on social media is like having a new pair of socks that stays just as fresh and snug as the day you brought them home. Imagine that! Although, I can't promise you won't lose a disinterested oddball fan from time to time.

Instead of fading socks that disappear through that secret dryer door that we all know exists, responsive communities really can continuously refresh over time: no more dingy posts and disappointing interactions (or lack thereof) on your social media platforms.

Here are 20 simple ways to maintain perpetual content freshness worthy of a massively responsive online community.

1. **Refresh profile picture, seasonally.** One of the reasons people become addicted to social media is because it's in real-time and constantly changing. We can't help but wonder, "What's going on over there?" Updating your profile pic, preferably in different settings, is a fun way for followers

to feel they're part of your growth. It's essential for fans to feel they're involved with your changes which further fosters responsiveness.

2. **Tell a behind the scene story with visuals.** Getting ready for a meeting? Setting up at a trade show? Excited about meeting with a new client? Update and share the story with your community. Sharing a variety of feelings with them allows them to feel they know you better.

3. **Simplify your product and focus on what makes it unique.** I know the 10 pages it took you to explain your product make perfect sense to you, but no one cares about that on social media. If you can't explain what you do on your social accounts in **one** sentence or less, we've got a problem. Find interesting ways to simplify your product/service. There's more than one way to teach people what you do/offer.

4. **Give something away.** It speaks for itself, and it's a fun way to drum up spontaneous interactions that result in one-on-one connections. But, know and follow platform rules.

5. **Test your ideas on a varied crowd.** Know your Target Market and create various personas. Then, talk to those people individually in blog posts, visual cues, and even in your advertising copy. Gone are the days that you are talking to a "30-year-old mom of two." We now need to know her like we know our sister and talk to customers the same way we speak to any other close friend.

6. **Bring your product to customers.** Why do customers have to do all the work? Take your product to the masses! I mean, don't show up at anyone's house or anything. But, do come up with creative ways to mingle with customers outside your traditional four walls. Pair up with the local liquor store to have a wine tasting/social hacking night. Or, a caterer could partner up with a local band to put on a concert in the park.

7. **Share a comeback story.** No one has it all together! Especially not me! And you know what? People like to know they aren't the only ones who don't have it all together either. We all have stories about how we almost gave up but persevered and came out on top. These stories are often the

catalyst to building loyal customers and should not be ignored or left out of your brand's story.

8. **Use fun graphics.** Fortunately, many programs have made it so easy to create fun visuals that ignite conversation. Canva.com just happens to be one of my favorites!

9. **Take in-the-moment photos/video.** Do you know what makes lifelong friends? Think about it; chances are your closest friends went through some pretty rough stuff right along with you. Siblings, battle buddies, college roommates, and workmates. They were there with you day-in and day-out, which fostered an unbreakable bond. Being in the moment with your fans does the same thing.

10. **Grateful attitude towards customers.** Say thank you! And find creative ways to do it. Social media gives companies the ability to be a little stalker-ish, so find out your fan's favorite book or team and send them something in the mail just for being loyal. Not one customer buys from you because they have to, so make your appreciation known!

11. **Refer Twitter users to TikTok videos.** Cross-reference good content that you share across platforms. Don't make it a habit, but if you have something good to share, share it everywhere!

12. **Use geotags** Enabling location services allows you to selectively add location information to your posts, which alerts potential customers in your vicinity to what you've got going on around them.

13. **Give credit where credit is due.** If you've been inspired, encouraged, alerted, or even had an idea that didn't originate with you, share your recognition in creative ways that are true to your branding voice.

14. **Plan updates ahead of time with a posting calendar.** Convince and Convert has a great article that talks about the importance of "visualizing how your content is distributed throughout the year." It helps create the consistency needed for fans to take you seriously. Download their free template and get started today!

15. **Become a community fixture without interrupting.** No one wants to be interrupted while they're busy enjoying life. But, if your product/service really will enhance life or even make it just a little bit better, it's important to find ways to tell your story to fans in a way that welcomes your presence.

16. **Understand your community impact.** Do you know how you fit into your community? Do you know your place in the hierarchy of your offering? It's essential to understand the where/when/why/how your community expects to interact with you.

17. **Have fun; be yourself!** Enough said!

18. **Make an unexpected partnership.** I touched on this in tip #6, but the Social Media Examiner recently shared an interview where Andrew Davis discusses lots of great partnership ideas! Look it up online for more details.

19. **Be confident and knowledgeable in what you post.** Please, only keep to the topics you know, those you can speak to confidently and back factually.

20. **Do what makes you happy without the pressure to sell.** I saved this one for last because chances are you skipped all the way to the bottom of this list. If you follow any of these tips, I'd say this is the most important one! When you address your social accounts with the urgency to sell something, it's the quickest way to suck the life out of your online presence. Represent your organization as if you're a philanthropist, and this is your hobby. Creativity will come to you in whole new ways that actually resonate value and interest within your community.

These social strategy aids are sure to get you "Made to Market" ready.

NOTES

Chapter 15

SETTING THE RECORD STRAIGHT

et's face it; this life is all about trials, trauma, and tribulation. But why, especially as women, do we let that knock us down and silence our voices? I believe that's a choice we make, and I refuse to play the victim. Since trouble is part of life, I'll embrace it.

Easier said than done, I know! But while picking myself up from off the floor at this very moment, what choice do I have. Pity? Doubt? Fear? Anger? What good will any of that do for me or anyone else who needs to rise up from a similar situation? As humans, I believe we are responsible for being an encouraging example to one another, so that's the framework from which I choose to operate.

While writing this book, I parted ways with my employer and left behind my hard-won role as Marketing Director. Why? Because I stood up, stood firm, and spoke out about the need to do the right thing. Obviously, the powers-that-be had a different opinion, and that's fine. We won't have the same views all the time. But what we do have, is the ability to do what's right – despite the fallout. When I talk about holding the ethical line, those aren't just words. When I speak about righting marketing wrongs, sometimes, it looks like losing your job. It's not pretty, and it's no fun.

I'm being transparent about my situation because I don't want anyone to say, "Sarah, that's cool you were in the position to walk away from your employer, I'm not." Well guess what, I'm not either. But what I can't do is be part of a broken system just for the sake of a paycheck. No matter how bullheaded it looks, I refuse to be part of the problem. Instead, I choose to devote my time and energy to the solution! Because if I'm not willing to stand up against deceit and encourage others to do the right thing along the way, then I'm part of the problem.

I wrote this book for a few reasons. Number one, I want to be part of the solutions offered to marketers to improve the industry as a whole. Number two, sharing the twists, turns, and stumbles along my professional path may encourage others to know that professionals hustling doesn't always equal having it all together. I mean, I can't be the only one experiencing ironic shenanigans that leave me in a constant state of reinventing and reimagining. Can I?

The irony is that I've been told only once that I qualify for a traditional marketing position and ended up losing *that* position while writing a book on how I got there! I mean, I know that's supposed to make me feel like a defeated failure who can't get it together. But I DO NOT! Instead, I feel liberated over the idea that I can achieve independence in this life and succeed at doing so!

It's what I started doing 15 years ago with Merrilee but was slowed by ongoing trials, trauma, and tribulation. Although progress decelerated, it never stopped. As you know, past events unfolded very differently than the dream I had in mind – but now it's all been redirected and reignited; revealing a new dream. So, I'll try it again!

I'm not broken, and neither are you!

I wrote a wildly different chapter for you here, but three days after losing my job, I knew I had to re-write this chapter to keep my story moving forward. Why? Because all I have is this moment, and I'll be damned if I don't use it to make a lasting difference for me, for you, and for anyone who's stumbling upon my story.

So, I'm using this time to shake things up and try something I've never tried before. I choose to use this opportunity as a chance to stretch my faith in God, my abilities as a marketer, and in building connectivity with humanity. I choose to take a blind step forward and let my unknown, hurdle-ridden path continue to unfold. But this time, I'm inviting you to join the journey.

Do you know what happens as a result of trauma? Often, we get caught up in our emotions and desperately seek out comfort. Nobody likes the fear and uncertainty of breaching a comfort zone and taking a risk. But honestly, where I'm sitting right now, that's the only way to go forward. Life has just shaken me to my core, but I choose to view it as a blessing from God and lean into what He's doing in my life -- free of fear! The only difference between you and me is I've proclaimed my stance publicly for all the world to see, and if I fail, I do it with everyone watching.

With nothing left to lose, why wouldn't I show up as my entire self? I refuse to show up as anyone else any longer. It's all or nothing because when I show up, I bring all of who I am. Even though I risk rejection, even in my brokenness, showing up as my whole self makes me whole. I can do that confidently because He who is in me has already overcome the whole world. So, there is no fight left, only faith.

And because my whole self is Made to Market, I will show up now, more than ever, and market the heck out of whatever opportunity is set before me. I will continue to use my voice for good. But this time, I'm doing it to benefit those who believe in me most. Whether that be readers, followers or clients. To you, I thank you from the bottom of my heart!

Once again, the rejection process I'm experiencing revealed how others see me. Surprisingly, it's wildly different than you may imagine. While friends and community members discovered I left the employment I'd actively and very publicly dedicated three years of my life to, one question was asked over and over again:

"What's your next adventure, Sarah?"

See, onlookers recognized that my last job was just a stop along my professional path, not the thing that defined me. If acquaintances and strangers showed up to remind me, I was destined for more, it's time I recognized it too.

Funny enough, my next adventure has been in the works for a little over a year. I just didn't see it unfolding until the veil of dedication to my duties was lifted, and I could see clearly.

When the wall looks too high to scale, that's when you know you have to start tearing them down.

So, what does all this have to do with marketing?! Everything, of course! I mean, when you are truly Made to Market, you find a way to continue—in the most creative ways.

Like you, I've also been asked many times how I coped through a Covid year. I always answer with—"Covid was a good year for me!" I know that's not your typical response but hear me out. Just months before the country shut down, I was promoted from Communications Director to Director of Marketing and Tourism. Being new to the role, the industry, and the area, I started a bit behind the curve. Immediately I sought out industry experts and asked them to train me on how to succeed in tourism. Incredible partners stepped up and showed me the ropes. Then, the shutdown. Just four months into my new role, I now had enough footing to begin executing as a true Tourism Director. But, being new to the area, I didn't feel like I knew the landscape well enough to tell a good story about why folks should visit Jackson County instead of neighboring destinations.

Thankfully, the Alabama Governor never shut down the outdoors. As long as we maintained a healthy distance, the Alabama outdoors were considered essential to maintaining positive mental health during an unprecedented crisis. So, I hit the ground running. Literally. As the third largest land-mass county in the state, I had a LOT of ground to cover. So, every week I visited a new outdoor spot. Some places were well known; others were hidden gems suggested by locals. During my visits, I brought everyone along through Instagram Stories, which you can find at @TrailTherapyAL

"Where should I go next?" was a question I often asked, publicly.

All year, adventure ideas never stopped pouring in. Still, I kept our 2020 advertising simple, with a full-page ad that could be converted for print or digital, encouraging folks to follow along on our outdoor

Instagram Story adventures. That year, our following grew by a whopping 200% as I soon became an expert on what our county had to offer. But I didn't do it alone.

An incredible opportunity to learn the landscape and spend time in nature.

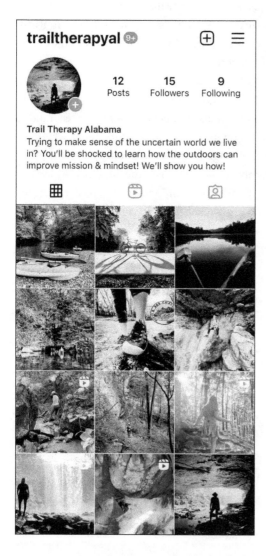

One of the tasks I took on as Tourism Director was updating our visual asset library. Before I came on, the same handful of tired photos were used to market the area for almost a decade. So, very early on, I began working with area photographers to build a massive library to create jaw-dropping visuals for the content creation process. Although I worked with several, only one photographer was willing to get out in the woods with me regularly.

Ashley, owner of Life's Mirror Images, not only became my trail partner but my partner in content creation crime! Together, we discovered a renewed love for the outdoors and told our story, one adventure at a time. While outdoors, we documented it all! From Alabama's most challenging hike—The Walls of Jericho—to discovering a waterfall trail that takes three days to complete. We found healing and happiness in the woods. I mean, we're just a couple of regular gals, so if we could do it, we should show others how to do it, too!

Did you know the outdoor industry grew exponentially in 2020?

- Paddling sales grew by 56%, reaching $172 million by June.

- Camping sales increased 31%, reaching $605 million by June.

- Road bike sales were up 63%, reaching $697 million by June.

By mid-summer, the world spoke, saying, "We want to go outside safely, show us where!"

If you were looking for a new outdoor experience in North Alabama in 2020, Ashley and I were sharing how, and in real-time. Our efforts resulted in our lodging tax numbers to reach close to 2019's total performance by June of 2021. That was a direct result of our early jump on the outdoor content creation process in a consistent, unique landscape.

It would have never been possible without our creative use of social media. Our videos were so well-received that it was not unusual to receive thousands of views within minutes of posting a new Instagram Reel. Viewers become willing and passionate spectators of our material and although the stories have disappeared you can view a condensed version of our adventures on my TikTok page, @SarahStahl4.

While visiting, you will see that the care and management behind a successful social media presence can be quite time-consuming. But when done right, it can make all the difference between stagnation and growth! That's why many leaders want to understand better how the cost of paid time translates into moving the organization toward intended goals. Ideally, every business action should have a tangible result. How else do we improve, grow, and outperform the competition? Leveraging social media is no different; however, as we learned earlier, it requires a different kind of analysis than used in the more traditional marketing measuring process.

Listen, it's tempting to throw up our hands and discount social as an elusive time suck. We're not doing that here because we know appropriately analyzed social media results are a powerful and effective marketing tool. But we have to be willing to do the hard work to see those results through to fruition.

75% of millennials' purchase decisions are influenced by a brand's social media presence, according to *2020 Animoto Data.*

Companies who continue making antiquated marketing decisions instead of listening to customers, will not see the growth they're hoping to garner from time spent on social. But it doesn't have to be that way.

By now, you know I've experienced a different reality through a story-focused execution on social media. The idea that a digital marketing strategy is a "useless waste of time and resources" is the laziest opinion I've ever heard about how to create results on the back of the most consumer engaging tools available.

So, what do results of a well-crafted social campaign, one that addresses the target audience's pain points, look like? Event sign-ups that result in leads, direct website purchases, post tags, shares and comments, increased story views, and even winning an election! Clicks are only vanity metrics when they're not tied to an action taken. But when actions are tracked and lead to results that support organizational goals, social media ROI is much more tangible.

It Doesn't Mean It's Not Possible

The beauty of a well-crafted marketing mix is it levels the playing field, but businesses have to know how to play the game and not be discouraged by their lack of short-term results. To play the game simply means telling your honest, ongoing story.

Companies that don't yet understand that customers are more important than sales will not make it through the next generation of business. Sales are the by-product of solving a customer's problem - resulting in a healthy relationship. You don't have sales without customers, and if you don't know how to communicate with customers, you won't have sales. So why push sales first? From where I'm sitting, here's where the problem lies.

What's the point?

Marketing has evolved to the point where the product and business personalities are one and the same. People no longer feel comfortable buying the product unless they can get behind what the business stands for. We see more product shunning now than ever, and it's not Facebook or any other social platform's fault. The fault lies in the marketing industry's ability to connect customers to products they can relate to. We must get back to being marketers again, and we can't do that without adjusting to consumer needs that evolve regularly in the modern marketplace.

The purchasing process now includes:

    1. Recognition of needs and wants

    2. Information search

    3. Evaluation of choices (research and review assessment)

    4. Purchase

    5. Post-purchase evaluation

A healthy purchase process is influenced, authentically. In a 2021 *Forbes* article by Danielle Wiley, Founder and CEO of Sway Group, titled, "Get More from Influencer Campaigns: The Secret for Extending ROI," shows how much things have changed since 2014 and how consumers' purchasing decisions are very much influenced by what they consider a trusted source.

The article kicks off with a bold statement of its own.

"Influencer marketing's popularity and demand show no signs of slowing down; in fact, it's been predicted that brands will spend up to $15 billion on influencer marketing by 2022. Influencer marketing keeps on outperforming traditional marketing, primarily because influencers understand their audience's interests and can bring brand messaging to life in a way that's relevant, authentic, interesting, and (ideally) doesn't feel like a commercial."

I know that influencer marketing has become a trend as of late, and rightfully so. The growing popularity of this rising star marketing feature is nothing more than *"The ability to produce high-quality, engaging content that resonates with audiences and perfectly suited for social media sponsorships."* The need to gain trust in a new market segment is understandable. However, this approach should be used as yet another tool in an overall integrated marketing campaign, not a singular strategy.

Although I no longer hold my former marketing position, I am pivoting to help others accomplish the content creation pieces that they know will elevate their travel brand to a whole new level. Follow us on the @TrailTheraplyAL Instagram Story to see how Ashley and I can make your travel brand "Made to Market" ready!

NOTES

Chapter 16

OKAY, NOW WHAT?

Remember all that summer raking I did? I didn't understand until I was an adult that I'd been focused on the wrong tangible. No doubt, because I was a child, my motives were silently and selfishly motivated. I wanted someone to acknowledge what I'd done! But really, who cares who saw? I knew I was doing the right thing, obeying my parents and working hard to exhibit the intense pride I held for my little corner of the world.

Think about it.

In one way or another, all of us are doing just that—holding up our own little corner of the world. But for what purpose? Are we relentlessly sifting through what's around us, cleaning up the fallen pieces and turning them into a tangible that makes us proud?

As marketers and business owners, have we really grown out of that? Do we have the maturity to truly embrace the consumer-centric emphasis we claim in marketing? According to consumers, we're not. Only 34% of consumers trust the brands they use, so we're clearly not delivering customer-focused marketing. We're still shouting, "Look at me! Look at me!" We seek approval and strive to win awards for all our hard work.

But what if our reward as marketers is nothing more than an uptick in overall brand trust from the ethical communications with customers we truly care about?

When I finally realized that I could manifest pride in my work through authentic connections *with others* rather than bragging *at others*, the little girl inside me grew up. Now, instead of building forts and hosting lemonade stands, I'm building businesses and better marketers behind the scenes, just as I was always meant to.

It strikes me how the act of raking, represents a "sifting through" process to uncover the best possible conclusion, has been a consistent theme throughout my life. That's how I know I am Made to Market!

Reading this book might be part of your own sifting-through process. Your timing couldn't be better! As you've seen, the industry is experiencing a seismic shift, which has created a marketing crossroads. So, which path will you choose at this junction?

You can stay on the well-worn reactive path of profit-centric mass marketing or help me and my cohorts pave a more proactive path to preemptive-based, consumer-centric marketing that results in clearly articulated success.

The reactive path was paved by marketers trying to figure out how to sell more to address lagging consumer response. In the meantime, customer attention shifted to niche marketplaces. Mass marketing got lost in all the noise, and we have reached an industry bubble that needs to be carefully deflated and redirected before it pops altogether. We must regain confidence and shift focus toward honing our ability to communicate, compel, and convert consumers in the new era of marketing if we're going to maintain industry buoyancy.

Where do we go from here?

What direction you take next will set the foundation for professional longevity. That's why we need to talk about Gen Alpha for a minute. Named after the first letter in the Greek alphabet, Gen Alpha's are born between 2011 and 2025, meaning that everybody was born in the 21st century, with most being children of millennials.

If we're concerned about the direction of consumer trends, we should keep our eye on Generation Alpha. *"They will be the most formally educated, the most technology-supplied, and globally the wealthiest generation ever,"* says Mark McCrindle, who researched and coined the name.

Also known as Generation Glass, they're expected to prefer the virtual world to the real one. With technological advancements such as artificial intelligence, self-driving cars, and other solutions that facilitate existence at their disposal. It's expected that Gen Alpha will pay even greater attention to self-care: mental well-being, hobbies, and other shades of personal development.

Given that the oldest Alphas are 10 years old, it's still too early to draw any reliable and long-term predictions about their consumer behavior. However, Gen Alpha marketing has already begun. Just watch and listen to how kids nine and younger respond to YouTube stars. Typically, in a one-on-one setting, children as young as five who watch gaming platforms are discovered to influence purchasing decisions based on virtually-based subject recommendations. Clearly not old enough for Facebook yet, will they ever plan to use it? Only time will tell how this new generation's web-based communication patterns will evolve.

When it comes down to it, understanding our newest generation is the type of insight that enables us to pivot and adapt to an experience-based marketing model that will soon dominate the marketplace. Remember, people don't just buy products; they buy experiences and emotions. As marketers, we must change our thinking from "What am I promoting?" or "How should I promote this?" to **"WHY am I promoting this?"** The global marketplace is heading toward emotional branding. We're seeing it now and in emerging consumer models indicative of the next generation.

How will we market to this new generation to capture and keep their attention while earning their trust? By telling customized stories about how your product/service relates to their specific pain points. Being vulnerable and transparent about what that looks like to your customer and bringing them along the growth process will be vital. Nobody can implement a better marketing paradigm than you! Marketers, you possess the ability to tell an ongoing story and then develop the strategy to deploy said story to a particular target audience. If you can't or aren't doing that, you should seriously reevaluate your position in marketing and what steps are needed to get you there.

The good news is, it's never been easier to get your story out there! The bad news is, it's never been harder to get people to care.

As an organization, you'll never receive peak performance results if you don't control your marketing strategy. The most effective marketers may already exist within your organization (or should be hired in) and are best positioned to tell your ongoing story to a niche audience – while tracking and articulating results. Or, they may need additional training to help them reach optimal performance levels. That's where I can help.

It's simple.

1. You have a customer, and your customer has a story.

2. You have a future in mind with that customer that connects your story with theirs.

3. You design a clearly defined path to build a future together.

Strategy development is that simple. Our job as marketers is to inspire people by linking our stories to help our customers change their lives based on a well-paired solution. There's no guesswork here.

It's much more compelling to say, "I've got a great story to share with you!" than it is to say, "I've got a great business I want to tell you about!" So, as soon as you develop your organization's story, tell it! Even more compelling, tell your customers' stories. The trick is finding where your organization and your customer's story collide!

That's why it's so important to get the story right—creating a clearly defined pathway for the ideal client that inspires them to invest in a better future. I've delivered every marketing solution in this book to help you become a better storyteller. These solutions reveal how to build, stack, and analyze content based on how the story resonates with the customer. All of these efforts work in concert to earn trusted customer relationships across every communication touchpoint at your disposal. On a macro level, you're ultimately contributing to the goal of creating a transparent, meaningful marketplace.

As of this writing, we're on the eve of 2022, and experiencing sweeping local and global changes due to the Covid-19 pandemic. At the same time, our world continues to evolve in technology, socioeconomics, climate, and environmentally—all influence consumer habits and, consequently, marketing.

No doubt, knowing what comes next is important. Using Gen Alpha as our guide is helpful, but it's a random variable, subject to change over time. As marketers, it's essential to consider and implement a foundational marketing concept that withstands the flux of change and time:

"Start with the customer and work backward!"

No matter where you look in business history, this simple message has been at the core of every solid marketing practice. We've read this message in books, listened to it on podcasts, watched it on videos, and even feel it as brands market to us. Yet somehow, marketers are always looking for the next best thing to make an extra buck. But if life has taught me anything, it's that the best option is to return to the tried and tested basics!

A universal and timeless edict bodes well as a default frame of reference for marketing:

Treating others with kindness, respect, and empathy will never get old.
Listening will never get old.
Personalization will never get old.
Meeting face-to-face will never get old.
Telling a good story will never get old.

Although many foundational marketing practices don't pack the same punch they once did, one-to-one personalization has a shelf life of forever! As we've discussed, as long as humans are the end-users of real solutions to real problems, caring for and winning the hearts of our customers will always be the most promising way to increase everything!

Today's consumers demand individual service and a personal approach. So, they appreciate when a brand goes the extra mile in customer service and communicates personal touchpoints - whether online or off.

That's achieved by continuously asking the questions you've learned in this book:

- What [specific pain point] is my potential customer experiencing because of [specific problem]?

- How does our solution better support, understand, and hear what problem our potential customer is experiencing?

- What is the solution, secret, or discovery to overcome the problem?

- How do we help overcome the problem using our solution?

- How does our mission, reason why, or inspiration behind the solution relate to this same customer?

- How is our solution a simpler, easier, and faster way to get results?

- Is our product the easiest way to overcome the problem?

If you can clearly define and articulate each of these questions, then you are on your way to being "Made to Market" ready.

Marketers - My hope for you is that you now have a clear, less overwhelming path forward. I hope you use this book as a reference guide to help build brands, tell stories, negotiate advertising, create content, set up analytics, and hold the marketing front lines with confidence. In time, you'll be able to develop a new breed of marketing that no longer compromises ethics or consumer trust.

Now that I've addressed the changing industry and its roots, I encourage you to stay ahead of the evolutionary process no matter what that looks like in your organization. You have what you need to build an interconnected and measurable content stacking process that aligns with a marketer's purpose. As a result, you'll better manage profitable relationships as long as your organization plans on being in business.

Employers – Your days of blindly hiring marketers are over! I've exposed technical insights by explaining the hierarchy of marketing, who plays what roles, and the knowledge and expertise required for each of them. Armed with this knowledge, you're now better situated to make your current marketing staff more effective! Just as important, you now understand the marketer's heart and mind, how they should be functioning, and their relational ties to other organizational departments, including your sales team. Finally, you've got the wherewithal to organize your marketing staff better and hire true marketers whose professional skills you can trust to build and grow your organization.

Now that you have a deeper insight into marketing roles and how they contribute to your growth process, you can create an effective vetting process when hiring full-time or contract employees for a marketing-related position.

What excites me most—no more hot summers alone with my thoughts! We can sift together to determine and apply consistent standards across the industry to ensure trustworthy storytelling is part of the marketing industry's future. That's our job as marketers, and we need each other to better understand what those standards are and how to uphold them.

Are you ready to get your team Made to Market ready? Get in touch!

Get in Touch

As The Social Analyst, Sarah firmly believes that marketing should be clearly articulated and measured, otherwise what's the point? Sarah helps professionals achieve marketing success by making sense of a modern marketing strategy. With a decade of experience in entrepreneurship and business marketing, Sarah provides expert insight into the current and future marketing landscape while providing practical takeaways that can be implemented immediately. As an innovative marketing developer, natural leader, and Army veteran, Sarah is in constant pursuit of pushing marketing standards beyond industry norms. Passionate about all things business for as long as she can remember, Sarah's relentless about applying her ever-evolving marketing IQ to forward-thinking business practices. Learn what makes her and you, "Made to Market" ready!

Dear Marketers, the world needs you to stop selling.

Stop ignoring it!

The Marketing Industry is not what it once was. The world has changed, yet we are still marketing nineteenth century tactics to the twenty-first century customer.

How 'bout, let's not!

I don't know everything, but I know Marketing and I'm on a mission to shake up the industry by getting the next generation of Marketers "Made To Market" ready!

VISIT MY WEBSITE
www.sarahstahl.com

VIEW MY RESUME
https://bit.ly/3mFWFs7

JOIN THE FACEBOOK GROUP
facebook.com/groups/183503553823094

in @Mrsdstahl

🐦 @Mrsdstahl

f @TheSocialAnalyst

📷 @Mrsdstahl

To hire Ashley and I for travel brand content creation, check out:

📷 @TrailTherapyAL

♪ @SarahStahl4